THE TACTICAL
1911

THE TACTICAL 1911

*The Street Cop's
and SWAT Operator's
Guide to
Employment and Maintenance*

Dave Lauck

PALADIN PRESS · BOULDER, COLORADO

Also by Dave Lauck:

The Tactical Marksman: A Complete Training Manual
for Police and Practical Shooters

The Tactical 1911:
    The Street Cop's and SWAT Operator's Guide
    to Employment and Maintenance
by Dave Lauck

ISBN 0-87364-985-0
Printed in the United States of America

Published by Paladin Press, a division of
Paladin Enterprises, Inc.
Gunbarrel Tech Center
7077 Winchester Circle
Boulder, Colorado 80301 USA
+1.303.443.7250

Direct inquiries and/or orders to the above address.

PALADIN, PALADIN PRESS, and the "horse head" design
are trademarks belonging to Paladin Enterprises and
registered in United States Patent and Trademark Office.

Visit our Web site at www.paladin-press.com

TABLE OF CONTENTS

Dedication

This book is dedicated to those who train beyond the quest for trophies in competition,
to those who relentlessly train to save lives.

Special Dedication

To Berna, Michael, and Christopher

ACKNOWLEDGMENTS

Dave Lauck and D & L Sports would like to express great appreciation to the following people, as well as those who prefer to go unnamed, for their invaluable assistance in completing *The Tactical 1911*.

Robert and Janet Finnesey for their encouragement to begin an ambitious project; Jack and Gina Harvey; Suzanne Devine for her expert computer and preparation skills; Lt. Col. Jeff Cooper; Gary Paul Johnston, Harry Kane, and Harris Publications for their photos, evaluations, and testing of D & L Sports products; all of the range assistants for their dedication to monumental range tasks at the D & L Small Arms Training Academy (SATA), including Clint Copping, Tom Eekoff, Doug Dinmore, Ward and Bill Hoblit, and John Kramer; NTOA and *Tactical Edge* magazine; Larry Glick; Cameron Hopkins; Dave Anderson; Scoot Farrel; Ichi Nagata; Layne Simpson; Paul Hanke; Jan Libourel; Jim Benson; Walt Rauch; Mark Lonsdale; the *Soldier of Fortune* magazine staff and related publications for coverage and evaluation of D & L Sports products; Clint Smith of Thunder Ranch and Massad Ayoob of the Lethal Force Institute for their support; Bruce Massau, Cass Landman, Kurt Johnstad, William Rork, Dave Pacanowsky, and Scott Glen for their dedication to the craft; the dedicated D & L Sports clients, who are more than good customers—they're good friends with a mutual interest in performance; the editorial and art staff at Paladin Press (Jon Ford, Karen Pochert, Michael Janich, Donna Duvall, Bob Newman, Fran Milner, Barb Beasley, and Elizabeth Barry) for their insight into the firearms field and the need for shooting information directly related to the defensive handgunner, as well as their publishing assistance; and the Quantico firearms training staff for their quest to improve performance and their selection of D & L products.

Photo credits and appreciation go to Ed Brown, Charles Karwan, John Larsen, and Erik Remmen of NWS Group-9.

PREFACE

This book was written as a guide to the selection, modification, and use of the practical defensive 1911 for the dedicated handgunner. It does not cover the legal ramifications pursuant to a defensive handgun encounter. The reader must understand that the use of lethal force must only be applied in defense of life. I believe that it is the responsibility of the prospective buyer of a defensive handgun to research the regulations and laws governing the ownership and use of a handgun in his or her particular state. Any improper use of a handgun, whether a result of ignorance, negligence, or criminal intent, should be dealt with accordingly.

The owner/operator of a firearm might at some time face the ultimate life and death decision: this fact can't be taken lightly. Should the prospective buyer of a defensive handgun be unwilling to make the commitment to serious study of the skills necessary to become a competent handgunner, he should fully expect to shoulder the responsibility for a possibly avoidable death, including his own or that of a loved one. If you do not intend to be an intelligent, responsible, safe, and law-abiding defensive handgunner, don't buy a handgun. I am providing relevant information about defensive handguns and handgunning, but will not accept any responsibility for the misuse or misinterpretation of any of the information contained in this book. You, as a defensive handgunner, will shoulder the ultimate responsibility for all of your actions.

FOREWORD

Not long ago, a veteran street cop in the Southwest said that the ideal police service handgun would be flatter than most modern autos to facilitate plainclothes or off-duty concealment; embody perfect ergonomics with a uniform, user-friendly trigger pull; have a user-proprietary manual safety like that of a Smith & Wesson (S&W), Beretta, or Ruger; have at least the power of the trendy new .40 S&W and maybe more; and have enough cartridge capacity, but not so much as to encourage spray-and-pray defensive fire. He then wryly noted that this ideal pistol already existed—since 1911.

The Texas Rangers unofficially adopted the Colt .45 auto almost as soon as it was introduced. During the Dillinger days, such gunfight-seasoned federal agents as Melvin Purvis, Walter Walsh, and some of Eliot Ness' "Untouchables" packed the government model in lieu of (or as backup to) the almost universally standard service revolver. By the late 1960s, entire police departments in California and elsewhere were listening to combat pistolcraft guru Jeff Cooper and trading in their Police Specials for Colt Government model 1911s.

In 1974, as a young patrolman, I became the first cop in my department to carry a cocked and locked 1911 in uniform. "He's a radical," they said. "He's a maverick!" Then, in 1991, I was teaching a class for the Washington State Law Enforcement Firearms Instructors' Association and, as I took my coat off at the podium, the Colt Government .45 at my hip became visible. I heard a young instructor in the front row mutter to the cop next to him, "Look at that old 1911! Hasn't this dinosaur ever heard of Glocks?"

The truth is that the 1911 is neither obsolete for its intended purpose—gunfighting—nor the mark of a radical. In many ways, its design is safer than many of the currently popular police handguns of the "point gun, pull trigger" persuasion, although its short trigger stroke may not be forgiving of inexperienced hands in a high-stress gunpoint situation.

As a supervisor in charge of firearms for two departments that had optional weapons policies, I allowed only those who could qualify "Master" on the range to carry cocked and locked single-action autos on patrol. The agency for which I serve today as a captain issues a double-action .45 auto. Had we been able to afford to issue D & L custom duty guns with Dave Lauck's unique, accident-resistant trigger jobs, it would have been different.

However, you'll note that the title of this book is *The Tactical 1911*. The tactical 1911, as used today by Delta Force, the Federal Bureau of Investigation's elite Hostage Rescue Team (HRT), and the Los Angeles Police Department's SWAT team, is most likely to be called into play when a sudden dynamic entry must be made with maneuverability demands that preclude an MP5 or CAR-15, and where the

The LFI Special was achieved by combining 1911 experience from Dave Lauck and Massad Ayoob of the Lethal Force Institute. This performance package hosts a variety of street-worthy options.

mission is to neutralize life-takers with swift, precise, and powerfully debilitating fire. The 1911 remains unsurpassed for this type of mission.

What about routine patrol and plainclothes wear? Dave Lauck is uniquely qualified to answer that. I don't know of any other man who has two decades of full-time police experience during which he carried a 1911, including uniformed patrol, plainclothes, deep-cover ops, and tactical SWAT assignments, plus extensive and successful practical shooting competition experience and the in-depth mechanical knowledge and skill to become one of the nation's premier pistolsmiths specializing in this particular weapon.

There are many fine makes of custom Colt and Colt-pattern .45s. As law enforcement editor of *American Handgunner*, handgun editor of *Guns*, and associate editor of both *Combat Handguns* and *Guns and Weapons for Law Enforcement*, I've been privileged to carry the Colts, Springfields, and Para-Ordnances produced by the finest pistolsmiths of our time. I've worn them on patrol and in plainclothes, shot and won matches with them, and kept them at my bedside to protect my family, but none were better than the Dave Lauck custom Colt 1911A1, which has become my favorite of the breed.

In 36 years of shooting 1911s, I've found none that better combined 100 percent reliability with precision accuracy and sureness of control, and a trigger pull that would be defensible in any court in the land without sacrificing the ergonomics that made the 1911 such a wonderful reactive tool for self-defense in the gravest extreme. The trigger is an integral part of a Lauck tactical conversion, and, in turn, Lauck's vast experience on the streets and in court, as well as on the ranges and in the shop, is the heart of his wisdom on this subject, wisdom and knowledge that eminently qualify him to write this book.

When you fight for your life, one of the few things you can control beforehand is your chosen equipment. When you carry a D & L firearm, you carry the confidence and knowledge of Dave's many years of experience of taking such weapons into the dark place of fear and ultimate danger, a place where he's had to use the 1911 to defend human life on numerous occasions. When you're alone in that dark place with something malevolent that wants you to die, that confidence is priceless and life sustaining.

The tactical 1911 is a topic Dave Lauck is qualified to define, let alone discuss. When he talks, professionals listen.

The book you're about to read is the distilled essence of Dave's knowledge and experience, wrought in printed words instead of steel, his usual milieu. Absorb every word of it. The day may come when Lauck's work on your behalf will save your life.

—Massad Ayoob

Someone once wrote that if man does not learn from history that he is doomed to repeat it. In the often controversial arena of tactical handgun selection, it is a case of the so-called experts not learning from history and, only through a process of elimination, ending up where they began so many years ago.

For those of us in the weapons training business, the last 16 years have proven very frustrating as we have been forced to watch teams and agencies chase their tails in search of the proverbial perfect combat handgun. For whatever bureaucratic or political reasons, those who claim to know what they are doing have ignored the recommendations of those of us with decades of serious gun time and continued to spend millions of taxpayers' dollars on solutions to nonexistent problems. Such errors as the FBI's short-lived move to the 10mm, which put agents' lives at risk, have only proven to highlight what we have known all along, that the venerable .45 ACP has been and still is probably the best choice for tactical operations.

It is with the above in mind that this book comes at a very timely point in tactical weapons training, since history has gone full circle and the lessons learned and taught by the pioneers of modern tactical training in the late 1970s are now being validated. To crown it all, we now see the FBI's elite Hostage Rescue Team selecting a modified .45 as their weapon of choice—a lesson learned by others such as LAPD SWAT and Special Forces Detachment Delta many years before them. The problem stemmed not just from the law enforcement and military special weapons community, but also the example set by International Practical Shooting Confederation (IPSC) type practical shooting. In the late 1970s and early 1980s, we were all shooting combat-modified .45 Government models, but then the gamesmen, along with the manufacturers, began the swing toward extended barrels and compensators. It was a sad day for the true practical shooter, because from there it was a dismal plummet into full-blown race guns, impractical holsters, smaller calibers, larger magazine capacities, hybrid ammunition, and bulky scope sights. Now, the shooting world has come full circle with the increased popularity of the tactical category and the reemergence of practical .45s with only the essential combat modifications.

The same is true in the special operations community. It has been only a decade and a half, but now shooters have tried the rest, often with disastrous results, and come to realize that the sage advice that we gave 15 years ago should have been heeded. The sad thing is that if they have spent a fraction of the budget spent on research, development, and manufacturing on nothing more than ammunition and training, they would now be much farther ahead of the game.

However, the selection of a proven weapon system alone is not a tactical solution in itself, but only a first step. With the move to a new weapon, there must also come suitable ammunition in adequate amounts, new holsters and load-bearing equipment, and the biggest budget drain of all: professional training in the use, maintenance, and cleaning of the weapon for optimum efficiency. Here again is where this book will serve as a valuable resource. Dave Lauck's experience as not only a tactical officer and a top-ranked competitive shooter, but also a gunsmith, will serve any team well in their adoption of or transition to the 1911.

Unfortunately, most agencies do not allow their personnel the time or ammunition to become proficient, let alone good, with a handgun, and training is often no more than a one-time deal with little follow-up. To this day, few police or military shooters ever shoot enough to graduate beyond the mechanics of basic shooting and more into the realm of truly advanced combat shooting. This ultimate plane of combat shooting cannot be taught. It can only be experienced, and then only after a lot of time behind the gun and personal dedication. Again, however, a book like this can reduce the necessary training time by laying a solid foundation and directing the shooter's energies into the most productive areas.

—Mark V. Lonsdale

Chapter 1

SAFETY CONSIDERATIONS

If you are the owner of a firearm, whether for sport, defense, or other purpose, you are responsible for the safe handling and storage of that firearm. The thought of being responsible for a careless death by your hand, or another's, with a weapon you did not properly store or handle, should be enough incentive to make you constantly aware of and strive for safety.

Firearms are repeatedly blamed for the results of human carelessness and criminal activity. Except in very, very rare cases, this is just a human trying to transfer the blame for his mistake or criminal conduct to an inanimate object. If we discount any possibility of mechanical failure with the weapon system, the weapon's owner has sole control over the safety of the weapon for himself and those around him. Following a few very basic rules of gun handling and storage can virtually eliminate the so-called accidental discharge. Information in this chapter will help readers understand that the accidental discharge is, in reality, a careless or unintentional discharge.

ALL GUNS ARE ALWAYS LOADED

If all weapons were treated as if they were loaded, no one could ever claim that they didn't know a gun was loaded. A weapon that is considered loaded must *never* be pointed in a direction that would be dangerous to any undeserving person or property.

ALWAYS CONTROL YOUR WEAPON'S MUZZLE DIRECTION

Never point any weapon (which we have already agreed is always loaded) at anyone or anything that you are not willing to destroy and take full responsibility for destroying. Know where the weapon is pointing at all times. Just because it is not pointing at anyone in the room you are in doesn't mean it is not pointing at someone in the next room. (Many walls will not stop a bullet. You should keep this in mind, whether you are at home, your office, or in a motel room.) You will be held responsible for the destruction your weapon causes.

Not covering any undesired targets includes yourself. Make sure your holster selection does not allow your own firearm to point at your own anatomy or at others while you are in various positions. (See Chapter 4: Holster Selection for more details.)

Eye and ear protection is mandatory for shooters and spectators alike. First aid supplies must also be available. Knowing the routes to hospitals and having cellular phones on site are also wise precautions.

ALWAYS WEAR YOUR SAFETY EQUIPMENT

A safe weapon, safe ammo, effective shooting glasses, and hearing protection are all mandatory. Don't skimp when it comes to your safety equipment; buy the best. Steel shooting has become very popular in shooting competition and training. Shooting steel can present unique lead-splatter problems requiring the best shooting glasses and common-sense range practices. I highly recommend attaching an athletic security strap to shooting glasses to eliminate shifting during strenuous activity. Your shooting glasses should fit snugly around your eyebrows to prevent hot glass from lodging between your glasses and your eyes. They should wrap around your face to minimize the chances of side splatter. The glasses should allow for undistorted vision through all corners and edges of the glass to facilitate shooting from all positions.

Hearing protection can be a bothersome accessory in some tactical situations. This is especially true for an entry team or precision marksmen who require full use of their hearing in tactical situations. A solution to this problem is modern electronic ear protection. Internal form-fitting ear protection is now available with electronic circuitry which actually enhances the shooter's hearing while providing harsh-noise shutdown when weapon fire or other loud noises occur.

DRUGS/ALCOHOL AND WEAPONS DON'T MIX

Having a firearms incident because you are under the influence of drugs and/or alcohol will not be a credible defense in court. (If you inflict unnecessary injury to an undeserving person because you are under the influence of drugs or alcohol, don't expect to get the sympathy of a jury.) Substance abusers should be immediately removed from any shooting organization. Tactical officers who are on 24-hour call-out should be committed to a nondrinking lifestyle to avoid receiving a tactical call-out page while they have alcohol in their system.

I assume the main reason you are reading this book is to further your knowledge of defensive handguns. I have yet to meet a person who can determine when the need for a defensive handgun may arise. Hence, most defensive shooters carry their weapons on a constant basis. This leaves no room for being under the influence of anything except good judgment. Competition shooters who enjoy going out for drinks after a match, or at any time, must make the commitment to go unarmed and make sure their weapon stays under lock and key.

THE OWNER IS RESPONSIBLE

You, as the weapon owner, are responsible for the weapon, its use or misuse in your hands, and for its falling into the wrong hands. Criminals who are ineligible to purchase guns will not hesitate to steal firearms from careless, legitimate gun owners. The days of glass display cases are over for the responsible gun owner. This includes the rear window display cases of many gun-rack-equipped pickup trucks, which display your guns to thieves. In these days of carjackings, some thieves won't wait for you to leave your vehicle before taking your property and possibly using it against you.

A quality theft- and tamper-resistant gun vault should be considered mandatory, especially in households with children.

Securely locking or concealing your firearms is often the best deterrent against them being stolen. I recommend a quality home gun vault complete with fireproofing.

Gun owners who carry a firearm with them while traveling or performing other daily activities are best suited with a quality concealment holster. The firearm that is always with you is never left unattended. The firearm owner who carries a long gun during personal vehicular travel is well served by a rigid, lockable, and concealable rooftop rifle rack.

Your insurance might cover the cost of your firearms if they are stolen, but consider the implications of your children and their friends having access to your firearms. Don't be responsible for a careless shooting. You will be the one who decides when your children get safely exposed to firearms. Until that time, lock them up.

KEEP YOUR FINGER OFF OF THE TRIGGER
UNTIL IT IS TIME TO FIRE

Keep your finger off of the trigger until it is time to fire. If this rule were observed more often, many careless shootings would be avoided. The finger-off-of-the-trigger rule must be considered mandatory whenever you are loading or otherwise manipulating your pistol. (See more on proper hand position in later chapters.)

NEVER LEAVE YOUR WEAPON UNATTENDED

You are giving a careless shooting an invitation to happen if you leave your weapon unattended. While some so-called authorities advocate leaving strategically located loaded handguns around one's dwelling, this is something you are responsible for. If residence security is a concern, it would be wiser to secure your house to the point where someone could not gain easy, undetected entrance. Early-warning security devices (which allow you to obtain a properly secured weapon if a situation calls for it) can easily be added to your residence. This would eliminate the possibility of having loaded firearms in positions where they could be obtained by children or otherwise untrained personnel.

YOUR PISTOL'S READINESS CONDITION
SHOULD BE A SAFETY CONSIDERATION

You should seriously consider whether you actually need a cocked and locked autopistol or loaded revolver around your secured home. Your family members' respective ages and experience may be a determining factor with regard to your weapon's readiness condition. The time it takes to insert a magazine into an autoloader and rack the slide might be worth the piece of mind if you have toddlers in the house, even if the gun is under lock and key (children have a way of finding keys). An unloaded revolver and access to a speed loader may be quite practical in some situations.

There are, of course, situations outside of a controlled environment where nothing less than condition one will do. Condition one carry of the 1911 is a mode suitable only for well-trained and experienced handgunners. It is the weapon owner's responsibility to determine what readiness condition is proper for him in a variety of situations and environments where a weapon will be present. A weapon operator also has the responsibility of personally checking the readiness condition of any weapon handed to him by another. A firearm that has been out of the owner's direct control for any length of time must be condition checked as well. Know the condition of every weapon you come into contact with by personally checking it.

PRACTICE SAFETY AT ALL TIMES

While at the range for live-fire practice, follow the safety rules and wear your safety equipment. Be sure the range is adequate for the firearms you are shooting. Make it a habit to always be sure of your backstop and beyond at the range; it will become a good habit. You, as the firearm operator, are responsible for the final resting place of all bullets. In a live-fire encounter, an innocent bystander might unexpectedly appear behind the adversary you are dealing with. Don't make a mistake that you will have to live with for the rest of your life. Be sure of your target and what is beyond.

ASSIGN A RANGE OFFICER WHEN SHOOTING IN GROUPS

When you are shooting in groups, assign a skilled range officer to keep things running smoothly and safely. Obey the range officer's commands instantly, for shooting requires concentration that may preclude you from noticing a dangerous situation somewhere on the range. Inquire about and follow directives about the range being operated hot or cold.

If you notice a new shooter who appears to be ignorant of the range safety rules, fill him in politely and tactfully, but firmly. Most new shooters are more than happy to comply with the rules if they are made aware of them. Should your range have a problem with an unsafe, unsavory shooter that cannot be cured by the range officer, I suggest you and your group leave the area immediately and have the unsafe shooter dealt with by the range operator.

DO NOT SACRIFICE SAFETY FOR ANY ADVANTAGE

Do not sacrifice safety for any advantage you might gain by shortcutting a safe shooting procedure. This rule, unfortunately, is too often violated in competition, as well as in live encounters. No prize is worth shooting yourself or another. Shooting yourself or your partner in a live encounter will reduce the odds in your favor.

KNOW HOW TO HANDLE YOUR WEAPON
SAFELY AND CONFIDENTLY

Hesitation from uncertainty or lack of confidence about weapon manipulation shows up dramatically on the competition range, and even more so on the street. Acquire the necessary training to become totally familiar with your equipment. Failure to do so might embarrass you on the competition range, and it might kill you on the street.

AMMUNITION SAFETY

Most handgun manufacturers do not recommend shooting reloaded ammunition. (Doing so might violate the warranty on the firearm.) Realistically, however, few people can afford to get the proper amount of practice without shooting less expensive, reloaded ammunition. Reloading ammunition is not something an inexperienced person can jump into overnight. If you're not an experienced reloader, or aren't willing to become one, leave reloading to the experienced professionals. Ammunition is a critical element in a reliable self-defense system. Poor-quality ammunition can adversely affect reliability and accuracy, and can be extremely dangerous. Either shoot factory ammunition designed for your particular firearm or obtain properly reloaded practice ammunition from a reputable manufacturer. Severe injury can result from using improper ammo.

Many people take foolish risks with reloaded ammunition. On multiple occasions I have seen shooters who forgot to charge a case with powder, got a bullet stuck in the barrel, and then attempted to shoot it out with the next live round. Don't be foolish or cheap when it comes to your ammunition. No prize is worth the risk of shortcutting your safety rules.

If you shoot reloaded ammunition with lead bullets, make sure your range has adequate ventilation, and also be sure to thoroughly wash before eating to avoid lead ingestion.

Whether you load your own ammunition or purchase new or remanufactured ammunition, each individual cartridge should be inspected prior to use. The ammunition should be individually gauged and weighed to ensure fit and function in your firearm. Obtain the complete weight of a cartridge and compare it with your other cartridges. Excessively heavy or light cartridge weights could indicate an overcharge in heavy cartridges or no powder in light cartridges. Establishing whether the cartridge case has a primer flash hole will not be possible unless you personally load the ammunition.

I don't trust any reloaded ammunition that I didn't load. Using improperly reloaded ammunition can be catastrophic.

SAFETY AND MALFUNCTIONS

There is a reason for every malfunction. If your pistol malfunctions on a regular basis, don't think this is something that must be accepted. Take it to a competent pistolsmith and explain the problem. Have the problem diagnosed and cured before you carry the pistol again. Reliability is the primary concern when selecting a defensive handgun; your life may depend on it.

Shooters should be aware of malfunction clearance procedures for use in the unlikely event that a properly modified pistol malfunctions in a combat situation. These malfunction clearances should be practiced with dummy cartridges. A properly modified combat pistol will perform with an outstanding degree of reliability. Don't accept anything less.

Should you encounter live ammo malfunctions during casual range training, don't disregard safety rules. For example, having a hang fire during range practice would require you to clear the pistol in a safe manner after waiting a safe amount of time with the muzzle pointed in a safe direction. The malfunction clearance section of this book (Chapter 7) deals with malfunction clearance under emergency conditions. Don't confuse range malfunction clearance with emergency malfunction clearance.

There is no need to excessively force, slam, or abuse your weapon, provided the proper malfunction clearance techniques are used. Don't override safety rules because you are in a hurry. The more you understand the way your weapon works, the easier it will be to keep it operational.

A variety of weapon malfunctions can be the direct result of operator error. A common example of such is when a shooter completes a reload but does not fully seat the magazine. The weapon fires the chambered round but does not pick up the next round in the magazine and the slide goes forward on an empty chamber. The next attempt to fire the gun is obviously unsuccessful. This is not a mechanical malfunction, but rather a shooter error. Shooter error is drastically reduced with proper training and practice. Should an actual mechanical malfunction be a recurring problem with the firearm, it should be detected during precarry test firing and corrected. Mechanical tools, however, can break occasionally. Be prepared with a backup.

Good safety habits will become second nature if all safety rules are always observed. Safe habits are extremely important in high-stress encounters. Unintentionally shooting yourself or your partner will do little to help you survive the encounter.

Make safety a habit at all times.

Chapter 2

SELECTING YOUR PISTOL

The very atmosphere of firearms anywhere and everywhere restrains evil interference—they deserve a place of honor with all that is good.

—George Washington

Sadly, the SA auto, though a superior weapon to any DA selfloader in nearly every technical and tactical respect, has lost its political credibility. This is unfortunate, but serves to underscore how much influence things like ignorance can exert. Even more unfortunate is the fact that police officers' lives will be unnecessarily lost because of it.

—Firearms instructor

WHY THE 1911?

This chapter will explain why my experiences have proven that the 1911 is the best selection as an all-around defensive handgun. However, I am not prejudiced against various other handguns and am fully aware that there are certain circumstances where a specialty pistol will fit the bill better than a general defensive handgun (For example, the S&W J-frame Bodyguard .38 Special revolver makes a fine pocket pistol. In certain circumstances, a person might want a pistol that could be kept concealed and fired from the concealed position, such as from a pocket or a purse. This pocket pistol would perform better from the pocket or purse firing position than an unshrouded revolver or an autopistol. The unshrouded revolver may have a tendency to hang up on the pocket or purse lining and give the shooter reliability problems. The auto depends upon the slide reciprocating to function the pistol for follow-up shots. Fired from inside a purse or a pocket, slide reciprocation could be unreliable. The Bodyguard would be a wise choice in this shooting situation, but would be a seriously lacking handgun as an all-around defensive pistol. The reader will obviously be able to think of other situations where different styles of pistols would perform better for a specific task. It becomes a matter of using the right tool for the job.)

I am also aware that a competent operator can be just as important, if not more so, than the selected handgun design. Some revolver operators outshoot auto shooters and some pump shotgun shooters outperform auto shotgun shooters, but these feats normally only occur when things go just right for the shooter who is using less operator-friendly designs.

There is no reason to handicap yourself when selecting a handgun design. The general purpose, all-around defensive handgun we will discuss here is the firearm best designed to deliver reliable speed, power, and accuracy in the hands of a trained shooter in a combat situation. Selection of a handgun for purely defensive purposes first, with all other uses considered secondary, would leave us with a choice from three basic groups of handguns: double-action (DA) revolvers, double-action autos, and single-action (SA) autos. SA revolvers should be eliminated from consideration as practical defensive handguns because of the time it takes to reload them. However, as many first responders know, the SA revolver is still often involved in encounters. Quality SA revolvers are available, affordable, strong, and accurate. Many are available in large calibers.

Pocket Pistols

The majority of pocket pistols can be eliminated from selection as all-around defensive handguns by setting a minimum acceptable caliber at .38 Special. Whereas there are pocket pistols chambered in .38 and larger calibers, they are usually lacking in effective pointability, reloadability, sighting, and accuracy.

So, a commonsense choice for an all-around defensive pistol boils down to .38 Special/9mm or larger auto or DA revolver. Considering an all-around defensive handgun chambered for a smaller cartridge is foolish because of stopping power problems. However, a subcaliber handgun may serve well as a backup weapon when a full-size backup is not practical.

Some alleged firearms authorities would inform the reader that, based on its simplicity of operation, a DA revolver would be a wise choice for the untrained handgunner. I say that an untrained handgunner has no business carrying a gun. You *must* be willing to make the commitment to be a skilled handgunner before acquiring a handgun, and you *must* fulfill that commitment before carrying the gun.

Elimination of the DA pocket revolver from consideration as an all-around defensive handgun is not a hard decision to make. Remember, we are looking for speed, power, and accuracy to make up our all-around defensive pistol. Simply put, pocket pistols are lacking in all three categories.

Medium- and Large-Frame DA Revolvers

Medium- and large-frame DA revolvers are the next category for consideration. They come in calibers suitable for a defensive pistol, such as .38, .357 Magnum, .41 Magnum, .44 Special, .44 Magnum, .45 ACP, and .45 Long Colt, to name a few. These calibers are more in the ball park. No one will disagree that the .44 Magnum and similar magnum cartridges are powerful, but how well can you shoot them quickly? Too much recoil for speed shooting should be a consideration in your handgun caliber selection. Although magnum recoil is not what it is made out to be by many gun writers and movie makers, rapid fire on multiple targets can be hampered by magnum recoil. I am not a believer in magnum cartridges for general defensive purposes because of excessive muzzle blast, increased recoil, and overpenetration. These factors cause the speed, power, and accuracy we are seeking to be out of balance. (Magnums could be a realistic option for campers, hikers, and officers in dangerous wildlife areas.)

I consider the originally developed 10mm auto factory loads to be in the recoil and overpenetration ball park of a "full house" .357 or .41 Magnum, thus making it a poor rapid fire choice. I am also skeptical of handgun longevity when firing a steady diet of full-power 10mm rounds at the rate that serious operators shoot (1,000 rounds per week being considered average). The reduced loading of the 10mm cartridge and the recently developed .40 S&W cartridge are simply midpower cartridges with less to offer than the .45 ACP. The overall cartridge dimension of the .45 ACP is also better suited to autopistol reliability than the longer 10mm and operates at a lower pressure than the .40 S&W. (The longevity of 9mm-sized handguns firing the hotter .40 S&W is also questionable.) The .40 S&W and 10mm may be ballistic improvements over the 9mm, but they don't have the excellent balance of speed, power, and accuracy that is delivered by the .45 ACP.

Standard calibers in medium- and large-frame revolvers are available, such as the aforementioned .44 Special, .45 ACP, and .45 Long Colt. These calibers eliminate the magnum's muzzle blast and minimize overpenetration problems, but they don't improve the slower reloading speed and limited cartridge capacity that the revolver is plagued with, not to mention that the ballistics of these cartridges can be approximated in an autopistol. (New DA revolvers have become available with seven- and eight-shot capacities, but they typically come in only .38 and smaller calibers to achieve that increased capacity.)

Speed loading revolvers with swing-out cylinders can be quick with full-moon clips, provided the clips are not bent, which causes slow loading and cylinder bind. Full-moon clips do not work well for tactical reloading, as it is an all-or-nothing loading. Using two cartridge clips makes tactical revolver loading possible but complicated. DA revolver reloading always puts the shooter in a position of having the cylinder open and the handgun not ready to fire. People who believe that revolvers do not have stoppages or jams simply do not have realistic field experience. The bulky cylinder on a large-frame revolver also hampers discreet concealed carry of the handgun. In the case of the large-frame revolver, such as the .44 Magnum, the gun can be downloaded with .44 Specials for general defense application and uploaded with .44 Magnums for big-game hunting. The revolver also handles most snake loads better than the autopistol, and it can be left loaded for extended periods without a concern of rotating magazine springs. These facts indicate that the revolver can certainly be a versatile handgun in specific situations.

When considering the revolver for your all-around defensive handgun, you should determine if you want to restrict yourself to the revolver's cartridge capacity and moderately fast reloading as compared to the large-bore autopistol's ballistic performance, additional cartridges, and faster reload ability. Provided you select a quality autopistol, the debate of revolver reliability versus auto reliability will not be a concern. Exceptional revolver shooters certainly do exist and they can sometimes outperform autopistol shooters while using a somewhat limited revolver, but these exceptionally proficient revolver shooters are the exception rather than the rule. Generally speaking, most shooters can perform combat pistol tasks better with an autopistol. A skilled operator with a revolver will obviously outperform an unskilled operator with an autopistol, but there is no reason for a skilled shooter to limit himself by using a less efficient tool.

Narrowing Down the Caliber

Whereas the 9mm, .40 S&W, and .45 ACP can each end a defensive encounter if properly placed, there is no reason not to choose the most efficient of these cartridges. The 9mm cartridge has a disturbing track record of failing to stop an attacker with torso shots, and the .40 S&W is a relatively new cartridge that probably has ballistics slightly superior to that of the 9mm, but the .45 ACP has been long established as a proven defensive cartridge. The .45 ACP is another step above and beyond the .40 S&W with its superior combination of speed, power, and accuracy, and it doesn't have a problem with excessive recoil. Therefore, provided a shooter can use the .45 ACP effectively, there is no reason not to select this cartridge over both the 9mm and the .40 S&W.

The .45 ACP starts out at a .45 caliber rather than being dependent upon bullet expansion for an effective wound channel. Recent developments in .45 ACP ammunition provide the defensive shooter with a selection of bullets that are not only reliable and accurate, but can be selected for the particular job at hand. (Individual shooters should determine the penetration requirements they may face in their particular environment and select their bullets accordingly.)

The final caliber decision is yours, of course, but thorough study of the problem you are trying to solve will probably lead you to the .45 ACP.

Selecting the Action

The next decision is between the DA or SA. The new fad in autopistol actions has been referred to as "DA only." In reality, these pistols fire with only one type of trigger stroke, but they are referred to as DA because they use a long trigger stroke similar to that of a DA revolver. They have been brought specifically into the police market because they are allegedly safer than other types of triggering systems. In reality, an unsafe operator will be unsafe with any firearm.

The major drawback with carrying the true DA autopistol, as I and many other serious shooters see it, is having two types of trigger strokes to fire the weapon. Provided you carry the weapon with the hammer down on a loaded chamber, when you draw the weapon it is necessary to fire your first round DA and then revert to SA fire. This makes it necessary to adjust your firing technique when you change from a DA to a SA stroke. (These types of autos may or may not have a manual safety or decock lever, which is typically poorly positioned and difficult to operate quickly.) Acquiring a precise and fast first shot requires the shooter to be able to manage a long and heavy first-shot trigger pull. Some instructors actually promote drawing and firing the first DA shot into the ground in order to get the pistol into its SA mode. This, of course, is absolutely the wrong thing for a defensive shooter to be doing in a populated environment. Once the DA autopistol has fired the first shot, the trigger stays in the SA mode until it is decocked and placed back in the DA mode.

Choosing a double action normally results in slower, harder to achieve first-shot hits for most shooters, and although there are exceptions, most shooters find that holding the sights on target while pulling through an entire DA trigger stroke is much more difficult than using a consistent SA trigger pull. The DA trigger also usually requires the trigger guard to be significantly enlarged to allow the pivoting trigger to complete its stroke. (Some manufacturers claim this enlarged trigger guard is to allow shooting with gloves. What usually happens when shooting a pivoting trigger with a gloved trigger finger is that the open end of the pivoting trigger allows the glove material to be caught between the bottom of the trigger and the inside of the trigger guard, thus binding the trigger stroke.) The enlarged trigger guard also extends so far down the front strap on the pistol's frame that it mandates a low hold on the frame, resulting in increased muzzle flip during recoil. A handgun design should allow the shooter's hand and forearm to be as close to directly behind the bore line as possible to minimize muzzle flip. (Minimizing muzzle flip allows for the sights to be kept on target more efficiently when delivering rapid-fire shots.)

The so-called DA-only autopistols give the shooter a similar long, heavy DA pull on every shot rather than just the first shot. Whereas it seems absurd to make the more difficult DA pull the only pull option on the newer autopistols, it at least provides consistent shot-to-shot trigger action, and consistency is very important when it comes to performance.

Glock autopistols offer a trigger pull that is longer than that of other SA autopistols, but not quite as long as the DA autopistols. The weight of the Glock autopistol trigger pull can be adjusted to the shooter's needs, and triggering the Glock is the same on each shot. The Glock, however, still retains a pivoting trigger, which causes the same problems to the shooter when firing wearing gloves.

The 1980s and early 1990s trend of DA and DA-only autopistols was aimed at the law enforcement community and was primarily based on liability issues. Administrators involved in making decisions on firearm issues critical to front-line officers are often sadly lacking in information and experience. The 1980s trend was to convince general American law enforcement agencies that a longer and heavier trigger pull would be safer in police encounters. It was certainly aimed at replacing the well-trained officer with a tool that would somehow achieve its own mechanical safety, as well as reduce training and ammo costs because of its allegedly superior design. Whereas "smart" weapons may someday exist in the form of handguns, they are not here yet. Skill and safety are still operator responsibilities.

Selling firearms to the law enforcement market has always been a lucrative arena for firearms manufacturers. Convincing U.S. law enforcement agencies that they were carrying unsafe firearms in this era of high law enforcement liability was obviously a wise sales move insofar as sales are concerned. What seems to have been overlooked by police administrators during this time period is the fact that firearm safety is primarily in the hands of the operator. (People who argue that departmental training budgets will go down if they choose a simpler point-and-pull pistol normally fall into the categories of point-and-pull handgun salesmen, departmental bean counters who consider budgetary concerns more important than the lives of their officers, or the uninformed.) Inexperienced decision makers also failed to realize that selection of a DA autopistol would itself provide unique safety problems. DAs rarely have properly located safeties or decockers and therefore encourage officers to carry the pistol ready to fire with only a stroke of the trigger. (This is the same condition in which most general DA revolvers are carried for police duty; the Glock is carried in this condition as well.) In all of these situations, the pistol can simply be pulled from the holster, pointed, and fired with a single stroke of the trigger. The pistol can then be fired in the same manner until empty.

This is a critical concern for defensive shooters and police officers alike. Arming yourself with a point-and-pull firearm allows shooting potential to be acquired by anyone capable of acquiring the weapon. Oftentimes guns are lost to assailants because of poor tactics, and other times it happens despite your best efforts to avoid the problem. That is reality, and that is why point-and-pull firearms can be so dangerous.

A manual safety device is a mandatory item for any defensive or duty weapon. While it might be easy to say that you will never let another person snatch your handgun, in reality it could easily occur. There are numerous documented incidents of officers being killed or injured with their own point-and-pull pistols. There are also many documented incidents of a duty pistol with a safety device defeating the efforts of a would-be cop killer from turning the officer's gun against him.

The same ill-informed decision makers who felt that a DA first shot would be safer than a properly set up SA auto failed to consider the fact that after the first DA trigger pull, the officer would be engaged in a firefight with an autopistol cocked in the SA mode with no manual safety engaged. Expecting an officer to decock back into the more difficult DA mode while in a life-threatening situation is unrealistic. I have seen officers go as far as holstering cocked and unlocked DA autos in order to avoid the difficult first DA shot. Holstering a cocked DA auto without remembering to decock it has been a problem with poorly trained officers, and unskilled shooters have been known to reholster with their fingers on the trigger of DA handguns. The result is a discharge when they push the handgun into the holster.

The standard DA auto and DA-only autopistols have simply been a bill of goods sold to the law enforcement community under the guise of being a safer handgun system.

To further claims of newly designed handguns being safer, a common tactic is to point out the exposed cocked hammer on a cocked and locked Colt single action. This feature can make the inexperienced and less knowledgeable decision makers who often inhabit law enforcement administrations nervous. What is not understood by, nor pointed out to, decision-making law enforcement personnel about the SA Colt in the Series 80 design is its multitude of mechanical safety devices. While mechanical safety devices will not take the place of responsible gun handling, those incorporated into the Series 80 Colt are very sound and still allow for top performance. This pistol incorporates a manual thumb safety, grip safety, firing pin block safety, half-cock notch shelf, properly designed rigid trigger guard, and a reliable disconnector system. When in proper operating condition, the Series 80 is totally courtroom defensible. It can't fire unless the trigger is pulled to the rear and the internal frame linkage moves the firing pin block housed in the slide. The firing pin lock system ensures that the pistol will not fire, even if dropped on a hard surface.

One of the major advantages the cocked and locked SA has over the DA is its ability to deliver extremely fast first and follow-up shots. This is because of only having to manipulate one type of trigger pull—a short SA pull the first time and every time, which allows the shooter to break the shots with minimal sight disturbance. This has little to do with the trigger pull weight, which can be adjusted based on operator experience and training, but the real advantage comes from the short, consistent pull distance.

A street-carry-weight Series 80 trigger pull of about five to seven pounds is both safe and reliable for a defensive 1911. While very light trigger pulls can be achieved on the 1911 and are preferred by some very experienced competition shooters, they are not necessarily desirable on a 1911 that is to be used for defense. Some insist on light trigger pulls for carry based on what others use in competition. Anything less than a solid four-pound trigger pull is not recommended, and shooters who believe they can't shoot well with a five- to seven-pound trigger pull are simply inexperienced at trigger control. It has been proven time and again that a five- to seven-pound trigger pull is not a deterrent to shooting well or fast. Furthermore, an item often overlooked by shooters who insist that they need a light trigger pull on a 1911-style auto is the fact that an increase in trigger pull poundage relating to the trigger return spring results in the trigger resetting more quickly. A trigger that resets more quickly not only allows for a quicker follow-up shot, but also for more positive trigger return under dirty or freezing conditions. On a defense or duty pistol, reliability must be maintained as the number one priority.

Under extreme conditions, reliability testing of the 1911, where the pistol is operated in complete filth, trigger reset failure is commonly the first item to cause a stoppage. This problem is minimized with a more powerful trigger return setting and maximized with a light trigger return setting.

The Test of Time

The properly modified SA 1911 in .45 ACP has repeatedly been shown to be reliable, safe, and accurate in the hands of a trained shooter. It offers a variety of advantages that make it my choice as the best all-around defensive handgun, and if you study the choices of the world's top pistol shooters and authorities, you will see how very popular the 1911 has become. The facts show that it has been a superior autopistol for approximately 80 years. During this time, the 1911 design has been perfected by those who recognized its design superiority. No part on this pistol has escaped the test of time; weak areas have been enhanced and retested until superb performance was achieved.

Caliber and Specific Model Options

The 1911 is available in a variety of calibers and some of the smaller calibers have gained popularity in competition circles because of their lighter recoil and increased magazine capacity. But remember that in a defensive handgun, the .45 ACP still features the best combination of speed, power, and accuracy. The .45 ACP also features a superior bullet diameter as a defensive handgun cartridge.

Choosing the 1911 doesn't limit you to one model of the pistol. The 1911 .45 ACP is available in the Government, Gold Cup, Commander, and Officers model, as well as several custom variations. Careful evaluation of the different models available will allow you to choose the best one for you.

The Government is a full-size model with a five-inch barrel. The Commander is the same size as the Government only with a 3/4-inch reduction in barrel and slide length, although many people seem to think that the Commander is much smaller than the Government. The 3/4-inch reduction gives you a negligible concealment advantage while, in my opinion, giving you a sizable disadvantage in pointability. The shorter slide length, when compared to the Government, also reduces the sight radius of the Commander and makes for choppier operation, which gives the Commander less of a margin of error during the feeding and ejection cycle. The sharp-stroking Commander is also more likely to crack the optional aluminum frame when used with full-powered loads.

The Commander can be tuned into a reliable and accurate shooting pistol, but I prefer to stay with a five-inch Government.

If concealment is a critical consideration, one could select the properly tuned and dehorned Officers model and bypass the Commander altogether. Even though shorter, the Officers has a fuller recoil-absorbing slide stroke. I have yet to see an Officers model frame fail. If you carry a full-size Government

The five-inch Colt auto with the professional model package applied.

The Colt Officers model with the compact custom package applied. Notice the reinforced recoil spring plug and barrel bushing.

as a duty pistol and do not have room for a second backup Government, the Officers makes a very logical choice. Plus, the magazines and ammunition for the Government will work in the smaller, more compact Officers.

The Colt Gold Cup has long been billed as the Cadillac of the Colt autopistol line. Many shooters have purchased this pistol in expectation of getting the best available Colt pistol, but it has several problem areas that do not lend themselves well to filling the roll as an all-around defensive pistol. The Gold Cup comes from the factory with Ellison adjustable sights, a moderate recoil spring rate, a long and wide steel trigger, and a target hammer/sear engagement. These and a few other minor items are why the Gold Cup has a higher initial price tag, but all of these options are less than desirable for use on a defensive pistol. For instance, the Ellison sights are fragile and have a poor sight picture and should be replaced with a more durable sighting system. The front sight is notorious for coming off during recoil (the front sight should be specially installed on the ribbed slide for long term durability, and the rear sight should be replaced with a more durable unit if shooting longevity is desired). The long steel trigger is heavier than necessary and can result in a trigger bounce problem during slide operation, but quality aluminum replacement triggers are available. The reduced hammer/sear engagement surface on the Gold Cup may allow for a lighter target trigger pull, but is unwise on a defensive pistol. The lessened hammer/sear engagement area in the Gold Cup's lock work also requires an additional spring tensioning device to assist the two parts in maintaining firm contact. This leads to more unnecessary complication in what could otherwise be a simple and reliable system and causes more small parts to be lost. The moderate spring rate should be replaced with one tuned to the primary ammunition you are going to fire. Shooting full-powered ammunition in a lightly sprung autopistol can result in unnecessarily battering the handgun. A shooter considering the Gold Cup should consider the fact that he is paying additional money for features on a factory pistol that have proven to be weak during serious field use. There is no need to pay extra for something you can have done properly the first time on a Government model without the additional initial expense of the Gold Cup.

The enhanced autopistols recently made available from Colt offer several changes to the original 1911 design. Sadly, these additional features appear to be a mass production attempt to supply what the less knowledgeable consumer believes is a custom gun. Some of these features include a flat top slide, scalloped ejection port, undercut trigger guard, and a slightly beveled magazine well. The flat-top slide is primarily a cosmetic feature that some consumers like. It does allow for cosmetically attractive custom sight installation, but really does nothing in the area of function. The enhanced model beavertail grip safety is a slight improvement over what has long been the factory grip safety on the Government model, but it is a far cry from a custom beavertail installation. (There is a substantial gap between the frame and the beavertail, allowing for the web of the shooter's hand to become pinched between the frame and the pivoting grip safety. The beavertail feature of the enhanced Colt models is certainly a mass-produced and installed feature rather than the fine line fit of a custom beavertail installation.) The lowered and flared ejection port is a step in the right direction for spent case ejection, but still needs modification to allow for live round ejection. When combined with an extended ejector, failure to make this modification increases the likelihood of a live cartridge having its primer impacted on the ejector and igniting *uncontained* in the ejection port area. This problem has occurred numerous times when inexperienced gun handlers attempted to eject live cartridges from the chamber into their hand. The unsupported cartridge case, of course, explodes in fragments in the shooter's hand.

Clearing a full-length cartridge with a bullet in place is a critical function of the port on a combat auto. In the case of a dud cartridge, it will have to be cleanly ejected and not stopped by a short port to allow the next cartridge to chamber. Cosmetically speaking, the ejection port cut on the majority of autos, as they come from the factory, are rarely straight or cosmetically appealing.

The magazine well bevel on the Colt enhanced model is another example of attempted improvements in mass production. The magazine well is radiused at the front rounded edge of the frame and slightly beveled approximately three-quarters of the way to the back of the well. This creates a couple of problems: sharp, 90-degree corners are left at the rear of the well where the square corners interfere with magazine indexing during high speed reloading, and radiusing at the front of the magazine well causes the lower portion of the front strap to be left excessively thin for 20-line-per-inch checkering. This thin portion on the front of the magazine well relegates enhanced Colt autopistols to 30-line-per-inch checkering on the front strap because of the existing thickness left on the bottom front of the frame. One solution for shooters desiring a properly beveled magazine well, as well as 20-line-per-inch checkering on the front strap, is installation of a custom magazine well, such as the Heinie premium grade, which allows for removal of the bottom portion of the grip frame and the thin metal area at the bottom of the front strap. This allows the thicker front strap frame metal to be checkered in 20 lines per inch. The custom magazine well then fills the void where the metal was removed and gives a full dimension magazine well without extending the length of the grip frame.

A feature that has proved quite desirable for those seeking the best handling defensive autopistol is the high undercut trigger guard on the Colt enhanced model. This factory cut can be smoothed and blended for a comfortable high-hand grip, which allows the shooter to seat the pistol deep into his firing grip when used in conjunction with a high-sweep beavertail grip safety. This greatly assists in controlling recoil during rapid fire.

The 1911 design, in my opinion, is superior to any other pistol design currently on the handgun market for use as an all-around defensive pistol. It has been in existence for so long that all of the minor idiosyncrasies of the design are well known by the competent pistolsmith. The aftermarket features available for this pistol have become quite extensive over the last decade and allow for individual customization and enhancement into what I believe is the best all-around defensive autopistol. I do not recommend that any 1911 or other handgun be used as a defensive or duty pistol without complete inspection, tuning for reliability, and thorough test firing prior to field use.

While some might suggest that I am less than objective when recommending the best all-around defensive handgun because of my being in the 1911 enhancement field as a profession, the truth is quite the contrary. I entered the 1911 enhancement field because the 1911 base pistol design has proven to be an exceptional design for a defensive handgun. My business was established to make a fine design even better. With proper enhancements, there is no autopistol design that can be handled faster and safer.

The reliability of mass-produced, moderately priced factory handguns has proven to be relatively consistent throughout the reputable handgun manufacturers. Whether handguns are produced in revolver or autopistol configuration from Colt, S&W, Glock, SIG, Ruger, et al, mass-produced handguns can all suffer from the pitfalls of mass production, which can sometimes be reflected in unreliability, inaccuracy, and cosmetic finish flaws. Addressing such problems with large companies can be frustrating, to say the least. The logical defensive shooter will test, zero, and tune as necessary all weapons before carrying them. There is no detail too small when considering your pistol's reliability.

When considering the testing and evaluation of handguns, especially newly designed handguns, in the firearm press, one must also consider the marketing strategy and number of advertising dollars a company puts forth to promote their particular firearm. Sadly, advertising budgets can sometimes affect the outcome of tests and evaluations. Large ad campaigns translate into big dollars for gun magazines, and printing negative gun evaluations can mean the loss of large advertising accounts. Experienced shooters normally see through the glowing reports of the latest miracle designs.

In my experience, none of the highly touted new designs have proved to be what I consider street reliable directly from the box. In an effort to keep production costs down, factories obviously don't expend a huge amount of time and effort on hand fitting for reliable and accurate function. Most companies do well at delivering handguns for the masses that are usually accurate and reliable enough for the average Joe at a moderate cost. Conversely, the serious shooter is not satisfied with anything but the best. This has given rise to numerous custom after-factory treatments for firearms, especially defensive handguns. Shooters who are truly serious about acquiring a top notch defensive handgun will take the extra steps necessary to enhance mass-produced factory handguns into the most reliable defensive handguns available. There are a variety of sources for these services for nearly all modern autopistol designs. Be sure your service source is one that specializes in reliable defense products, not simply competition firearms. Hard-core reliability is number one, followed by accuracy and cosmetic appearance. The sources for enhancing 1911 autopistols have never been better than at present. Establishing yourself, your department, or your military unit with a reputable enhancement service can allow you to select the 1911 without hesitation and know that your selection will be serviceable for years to come.

If you objectively test available handgun designs in realistic combat/defensive handgun scenarios, I think you will agree that the properly set up 1911 is your best choice. Consider that, in 1910, the U.S. Military Board of Ordnance evaluated the design by subjecting the pistol to rigorous tests, including endurance, accuracy, rapid fire, penetration, extreme climate conditions, and mud and sand reliability. The Colt 1911 was determined to be a superior pistol after having fired 6,000 rounds without a malfunction or parts breakage. The pistol has been improving ever since.

WEAPON RETENTION FACTORS IN THE 1911

Many of us can recall being called radicals and mavericks when we chose to carry a semiautomatic pistol like the 1911 on duty instead of the then-customary police service revolver. Today, of course, the majority transition to the semiautomatic service pistol of the United States' 600,000 police is an accomplished fact. Unfortunately, many of the guns were acquired for the wrong reason, and their use was incorrectly taught, in some respects, with the result that while many officers were saved, still more who could have been saved were not.

Historically, autoloaders were purchased for cartridge capacity and speed of reloading to achieve parity with heavily armed dope dealers in a perceived firepower race. Once the guns were in service, it quickly became apparent to any unbiased professional reviewing the real-world field results that the autoloaders had two advantages of far greater importance than firepower.

Cardinal among these was improved hit potential under stress. The autopistol was unquestionably more ergonomic. The shorter, easier pull of the typical semiauto pistol resulted in a gun less prone to being jerked off target in the hands of an officer caught up in fight-or-flight reflex, his or her strength increasing dramatically even as his or her coordination plunges drastically.

It is worth noting that the 1911 was particularly successful in this respect. One string of Colt .45 auto shootings I tracked during research for *The Semiautomatic Pistol in Police Service and Self Defense* resulted in 100 percent hits delivered by the stressed cops and armed citizens who had been forced to shoot armed criminals. LAPD's elite SWAT team has issued Colt .45 autos since that unit's inception and had an overall hit rate of well over 80 percent in actual gunfights, including a long string of 100 percent hits, at a time when cops in other departments with other handguns were averaging around 25 percent hits in street shoot-outs. During that same period, even the "can't miss" 12-gauge shotgun was generating only 58 percent hits in the hands of highly trained LAPD field personnel.

The second major life saver, more important by far than firepower, was proprietary nature to the user. A proficient shooter knows how to operate his equipment. If a gun snatcher does not, that is fine. A history written in blood teaches us that whenever a cop faces a potential criminal, there is a loaded gun present: the cop's.

Consider the following facts:

- During one tragic string of cop killings on the Los Angeles County Sheriff's Department when .38 revolvers were standard issue, approximately half of the slain officers were killed with their own guns. This death toll was dramatically reduced when Sheriff Sherman Block transitioned his officers to semiautomatic pistols and required them to be carried on safe.
- Through much of the epoch of modern policing, an average of one police officer out of every five slain was killed with a snatched police weapon. This average has been greatly reduced by several factors, including police body armor of the soft concealable type pioneered by Second Chance's Richard Davis, snatch-resistant holsters, the street-proven and widely adopted handgun retention techniques pioneered by Jim Lindell of Kansas City, increased use of backup handguns by police, and, without question, the greater prevalence of semiautomatics with manual safety levers.
- In the history of the Hartford, Connecticut, police department, one of the nation's oldest law enforcement agencies, every officer murdered in the line of duty was slain with a police weapon snatched from him or a partner. That trend reversed after the department adopted a .45 auto with a manual safety.

More such saves are logged every year. Most are with S&W and Beretta pistols, the two most popular brands among police, which offer manual safety catches as an option. An advantage of the 1911 is that the manual safety is not optional; the gun has to be carried cocked and locked—with *locked* being the operative term—for safety.

Many instructors don't find the slide-mounted safety/decock lever of the popular DA service pistol ergonomic to operate or even reach. Some don't even know how to properly take such a weapon off safe. Since 1911, however, literally millions of U.S. soldiers and countless police officers and armed citizens have learned that the frame-mounted safety of 1911 pistols bore the same stamp of user friendliness as the other key elements of John Browning's ingenious design. Flexor muscles are stronger than extensor muscles, and with minimum training, any user of the 1911 quickly learns to wipe the safety of the weapon down into the fire position as a strong, fighting grasp of the weapon is acquired and the operator is ready to fire. This is one reason why, in the history of the speed shooting and replicated gunfighting developed by Jeff Cooper back in the 1950s and at the height of its popularity today, the supposedly ancient 1911 has reigned supreme. More to the point, it is one reason why so many professionals consider the 1911 the best pure gunfighting pistol ever developed, particularly when it must be used in a reactive, defensive mode.

Is a safety catch more important than firepower? The proof is on the street. As early as the 1970s, I was able to review the files of the Illinois State Police, whose 1967 adoption of the S&W Model 39 9mm made them the first major American law enforcement agency to adopt a semiautomatic pistol. I couldn't find a single case of a trooper getting hurt, let alone killed, because he was armed with an autoloader instead of the then-standard revolver. I did document approximately a dozen cases of troopers surviving life-threatening assaults because they had an auto instead of a six-gun. Four of those cases were firepower saves. In one incident, two troopers survived (and killed their heavily armed assailant) with more than 20 shots fired and speed reloading a critical factor. In another, the seventh shot put down a charging, shotgun-armed attacker. The fourth trooper was saved when either the seventh or eighth shot he fired killed a man who had already shot another cop and was rushing in to murder him. These last two were fast-moving cop-kill attempts that allowed no time to reload.

All of the remaining cases were weapon design saves. In some cases, the suspect gained control of the weapon, pointed it at one or more lawmen, pulled the trigger, and did no harm because he was, in every case, unable to find the safety catch to get the gun off safe.

There are fewer police saves on record with the 1911 for three reasons. First, of course, fewer cops carry 1911 pistols and therefore they are less represented numerically in such incidents. Second, a disproportionate number of those who do carry them are tactical team officers in situations where someone going for the policeman's gun is likely to be shot to death before he ever gains control of it. And third, it is entirely possible that because the 1911 pistol today is seen as the mark of the professional, the officer who carries one is probably more highly trained and aware than the rank and file, and therefore less likely to allow such a situation to germinate in the first place.

But it does happen. In one case in the Pacific Northwest, an officer was disarmed of his cocked and locked Colt .45 and the suspect tried to shoot him several times. The gun wouldn't fire and the perp fled. The deputy in question flagged down a passing motorist and initiated a pursuit, commandeering not only the car but the citizen's licensed .38 revolver. When the pursuit ended, the deputy made a successful gunpoint arrest without bloodshed; the suspect had not yet figured out the Colt's thumb safety.

Dave Lauck has been instrumental in converting many defensive shooters, cops, and sport shooters to the 1911 based on the pistol's ability to allow dedicated shooters to achieve superior performance. Contrary to what the less knowledgeable like to promote, safety, especially in the Series 80 pistols, is an integral part of the 1911 design. Most importantly is its field practical safety, which still allows the skilled operator to deliver rounds on target with unsurpassed speed.

The closest I've heard of a cop getting killed with his own 1911 pistol occurred in Florida, where the patrolman with the Colt .45 faced a true policeman's nightmare, a for-real professional hit man who was armed with his own Browning Hi-Power mounted with a high-tech silencer. In the course of the struggle the suspect lost the use of his Browning, but gained control of the cop's Colt. He was apparently familiar with guns and knew that the safety operated the same as on his own weapon. In the course of the struggle, the officer pressed the release and dumped the magazine, and ducked as the suspect fired at him with the one shot that was left. The bullet missed. The hit man's second pull of the trigger caused a harmless click. He fled; the officer survived.

The safety catch on the ergonomic 1911 can allow a faster draw. The reason is that the cop who knows the suspect will have to do something he doesn't expect to have to do (shoot the officer with his own gun) can carry his weapon in a faster access holster. Personally, during the many years I carried a 1911-style semiauto cocked and locked .45 auto on duty, my uniform holster was usually a simple thumb-break that allowed extremely quick access. With a point-gun pull-trigger weapon, I wanted nothing less than the most secure uniform holster available, which was usually a bit slower.

Maximum insurance against being killed with one's own weapon includes wearing body armor that can defeat your own ammunition. Many such saves have been logged by high-quality body-armor companies. Learning the most proven weapon retention skills is critical, too. Carry a second weapon; the practice has saved the lives of many disarmed officers and at least a couple of law-abiding citizens whose primary carry guns were snatched by offenders. A security holster doesn't do it by itself, but it's a safety net for when your hands are tied up fending off Suspect A and Suspect B has an unobstructed second or two to grab at your gun.

In the event your handgun is acquired by an assailant, a manual safety catch may provide you with enough time to implement effective countermeasures. Obviously, the user needs to be able to activate the safety quickly when shooting in reactive self-defense. This takes technique and repetition. There's no free lunch, but the 1911 provides the ergonomics required for safe, high-speed operation by skilled operators.

The bottom line is that the thumb safety design of the 1911 is a proven life saver, one of the things that makes it a tactically sound design in highly skilled hands. It's one reason why so many professionals, if given a choice, will select a tactical 1911 as their personal defensive handgun.

—Massad Ayoob

Chapter 3

MODIFICATIONS TO THE 1911

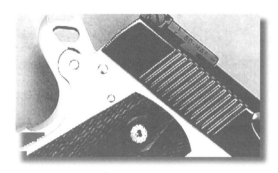

Oppressors can tyrannize only when they can achieve a standing army, an enslaved press, and a disarmed populous.

—James Madison

Accessories and modifications available for the 1911 are wide ranging. Therefore, serious thought must be put into which modifications will be right for your needs. Some modifications are considered essential to the 1911 for reliability and shootability reasons. Others are desirable, and others still are simply worthless gadget gun options not even suited to informal competition shooting.

I hope to shed some light here on what options will serve your needs best, making the main goal of this chapter to deliver information relevant to the defensive handgun, rather than the handgun modified for competition-only purposes.

PISTOLSMITHS

Selection of a craftsman to perform the work for you who is knowledgeable of the 1911 is just as important, if not more so, as selecting the modifications to be performed. The selection must be made on performance and not personality. Many base firearms have been ruined beyond the point of repair by friends practicing their underdeveloped skills on a handgun owned by another. You will be betting your pistol's reliability on your choice of pistolsmith.

I have examined the work of many pistolsmiths and have come to the conclusion that there are only a select few whom I would credit as 1911 craftsmen. It seems obvious that many pistolsmiths have never had to actually depend upon a firearm's reliability in a live encounter.

Prices charged by the top pistolsmiths are usually relatively similar, so cost alone should not be the determining factor of where your pistol work is performed. A long-term reputation for quality work, reliable, accurate performance, and service after the sale is much more important than a few dollars. Generally speaking, you get what you pay for. Exceptionally low pistolsmithing prices should be approached with caution. A good overview of established smithing operations can be obtained by reviewing which are members of the American Pistolsmith's Guild, the American Gunsmithing

Association, and American Handgunners Club 100. Although simply because a smith is a member of these organizations does not ensure perfection, it is a good indication that the smith is established.

Don't be surprised if a smith has a substantial amount of legal jargon in his literature about no warranties, no liability accepted, agreement not to sue, etc. Self-defense encounters have a good potential for lawsuits and a smith specializing in defensive equipment must have some protection from legal actions. Occasionally the smith may encounter an unethical client seeking an easy mark. Business done on a personal basis may provide that mark if business self-defense disclaimers and agreements are not in place.

True craftsmanship and customer service come from the individual smith dedicated to his craft and client. Backing one's services after the sale is simply a personal policy that the smith's reputation is built on. Personal dedication to customer satisfaction cannot be contained on a warranty card; it comes from a caring craftsman. Make sure your smith has this type of dedication.

The increase in popularity of combat-style shooting matches and carrying a handgun for self-defense has led to a substantial backlog of work for reputable pistolsmiths and has brought about some semi-production-line pistolsmithing businesses. The semi-custom production-line style of pistolsmithing may limit your options, whereas the true custom-built pistol commonly allows individual quality options to be selected on a case-by-case basis. More importantly, the owner of the pistol to be customized may never have any direct contact with the smiths working on a production line. This eliminates the one-on-one relationship between client and pistolsmith. I firmly believe that if a pistol owner is going to have a handgun customized he needs to speak directly with the pistolsmith doing the modifications. This makes the chance of an incorrect order extremely unlikely. It also gives the pistol owner the opportunity to solicit modification advice based upon the pistolsmith's experience. I believe this is a cornerstone in establishing long-term customer satisfaction and a reputation of quality service. Without a doubt, a pistolsmithing operation is a busy environment, but if the pistolsmith is too busy to speak with you about your order before the sale, you can plan on him to be much too busy to speak with you regarding any problems with the work after the sale.

MINIMUM 1911 MODIFICATIONS

Most knowledgeable 1911 pistolsmiths offer a basic reliability package including features that the individual smith feels are essential on any defensive auto. Some smiths prefer to keep their basic reliability package very basic, whereas others suggest a slightly more extensive package as the minimum for a defensive auto. Each smith has his own preferences based on his experience and should be able to articulate why he prefers to do things a certain way. I prefer a slightly more extensive basic pistol package to ensure all basic functions are covered the first time and that it will not be necessary to do additional work at a later time, unless I decide I want additional options. Having the complete job done right the first time is no doubt the best way to go. Working on the pistol after it has had the final finish applied will often require removing the finish in select areas on the pistol and leaving bare metal exposed to the elements, or incurring the cost of refinishing the gun a second time. Consider all of the modifications you are interested in, get them done the first time, and have a quality finish applied. Do not be penny-wise and pound foolish.

Basic 1911 performance packages should at least include the following:

- ruggedly installed, low-profile, high-visibility fixed sights
- extended, contoured thumb safety
- extended ejector
- combat trigger job
- beveled magazine well

Above, l to r: the MMC adjustable sight with protective ears and night sight inserts, Novak low-mount sight, Heinie fixed sight, competition model, and Bo-Mar adjustable.

Left: the properly modified 1911 is very accurate.

- polished feed ramp and throated barrel
- lower and open ejection port
- proper heavy duty recoil spring and shock buff
- polished and adjusted extractor
- heavy duty firing pin spring
- solid barrel bushing
- overall inspection for fit and function
- honing of critical areas for smooth function
- test firing for point-of-impact and reliability with proper ammunition

There should be a clear purpose for each reliability modification. To perform its intended function, each option needs to be professionally completed and fitted to the individual pistol. Beware of parts that are marketed as drop-in with no gunsmithing required. For the most part, these parts are poorly designed, and individual pistol hand fitting is a requirement for the utmost in reliability. The drop-in versions of parts are typically designed for quick sale rather than solid reliability.

Sights

High-quality, low-profile, high-visibility fixed sights are a necessary modification. Originally, the 1911 was issued with extremely small and hard to see fixed sights. They had to be replaced with larger sights to be visible in high-speed combat situations. Later models of the 1911 have improved sight size and configuration, but still have a bad habit of not standing up to recoil. This is especially true of factory front sight installations. Rugged installation of the sights is certainly necessary on a combat pistol, which will fire many thousands of full-power loads. This is particularly the case when night

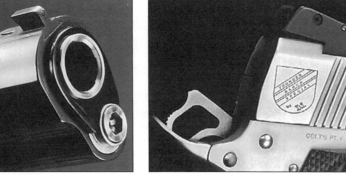
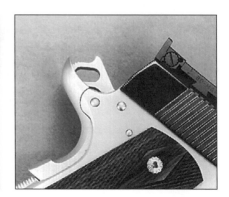

A recessed protected muzzle, two-piece guide rod, front sight serrations, and lengthwise dovetail undercut front sight.

Above center and above right: the excellent MMC protected adjustable sight and the Bo-Mar adjustable sight.

inserts are fitted into the sights, as losing the sight on the range can also mean losing an expensive night insert.

Consistent delivery of accurate shots requires using sights at all but the closest of distances. Low-profile sights tend to be much more rugged and snag-free when carried concealed. They are also less prone to cut the operator's hand. It should be mandatory for the sights to give a clear, crisp sight picture. Poor quality cast sights are available from many manufacturers and are not recommended. Cast sights commonly shear off the slide during recoil. Machined steel sights that are professionally installed should be considered mandatory. Shooters who have gone through the problem of losing their sights in the field, whether in tactical situations or competition, are aware of the problems in hitting their target as a result.

There are a variety of sight pictures available from fixed sights on the modern 1911 sight market. When choosing your sights, consider whether you might later install night sight inserts. Keep in mind that some sights do not offer the proper shape or dimensions to accept night inserts. Choosing the wrong sights and later deciding that night sight inserts are desirable will require replacing the base sights.

Most experienced shooters have gotten away from colored inserts and gone to straight black sights. My choice is straight black steel sights with night inserts. This is the more expensive route to take, but also the one that delivers the best performance. Some shooters prefer to go with three white dots on their iron sight system. This gives the shooter quicker sight pickup in low light without the expense of night sights. I have found the white dots to be ineffective in very low light and total darkness, and debatable in bright sun. The black-on-black steel sights give a black, crisp sight picture in daylight conditions, and night inserts allow for easy sight alignment in low light conditions. It is possible to install night inserts inside of white circles on some sights to give the three-white-dot effect in dim light and glowing sights in the dark.

The configuration of the front and rear sights should also be a consideration when selecting your 1911 iron sight system. A low-mounted, snag-free, yet highly visible rear sight makes concealed carry of the 1911 much more practical. The high-mounted fixed or adjustable sight adds unnecessary sharp edges to the top of the slide. The undercut front sight allows for a black front sight face under almost all lighting conditions, and it shadows out glare from light coming from almost any direction. The drawback to the undercut front sight, in some people's opinion, is that it is sharp and snag prone during the draw, and this is true, meaning that the shooter will have to use the proper holster with the correct depth of sight track. Such a holster will allow use of the undercut front sight without skinning leather or other holster material and interfering with the sight picture. The undercut front sight would not be a good choice for those who do not carry their pistol in a holster, as without a sight track the sight could easily create snagging problems.

I have developed a lengthwise dovetail front sight that can be cut into a ramp, post, or undercut front sight. The reason the lengthwise dovetail front sight is preferred over the cross-dovetail front sight is that it blends with the lines of the slide, and the rear portion of the lengthwise dovetail sight can be rigidly anchored all the way through the slide. This style of sight is, without question, ruggedly installed and recoilproof. In situations where a pistol retention concern exists, the securely anchored lengthwise dovetail front sight with an undercut post provides an additional benefit by being extremely sharp and acting as a substantial

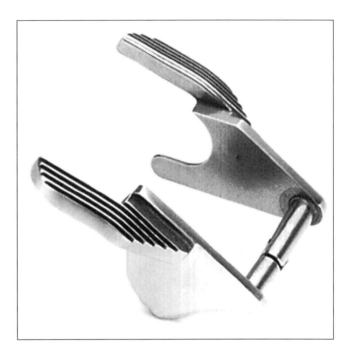

An Ed Brown ambidextrous tactical thumb safety with the levers narrowed for easier concealed carry. Note the joint joining the levers.

deterrent to a pistol grabber. Jerking the pistol away from a gun grabber with this type of sight could very easily take a meat sample from the pistol grabber's hands. This may be an important issue in a later court action, giving indication as to whether the attacker grabbed the pistol. I have used this sight for years with extremely reliable performance. A person will have to determine if this sight will fit his needs best, because it will require a holster with a sight track and additional machining fees to install it in the slide.

An improved ramp front sight and night sight post have become about the most popular front sights on the 1911. These sights offer a sharp sight picture and have little chance of snagging. Should you decide to have the pistol finished in a light-colored finish, such as hard chrome, be sure to advise your pistolsmith that you would like the sights to retain a black visible sight picture. This normally means sight installation after the hard-chroming process. With certain sights machined into the slide, the rear face can be blued after the body of the sight is chromed along with the slide.

Safeties

An extended thumb safety should be included as a basic reliability feature on a 1911. Such a safety allows the shooter to positively activate the safety in all conditions. The stock 1911 thumb safety is quite small and can be missed when shooting at high speeds or with gloves on. Extended, extra large thumb safeties may be acceptable on competition-only pistols, but you do not want to overdo the size of the safety on a defensive pistol. The safety should not be so big as to cause it to be brushed off during concealed carry. An enlarged thumb safety contoured to the individual pistol allows the best of both worlds—quick manipulation without being snag prone. The final dimension of the contoured extended safety will not be substantially larger than the stock safety, but rather just large enough to make its operation positive.

Holster selection is critical when a 1911 has an extended thumb safety. Some holsters with straps that go between the hammer and the slide can interfere with the thumb safety remaining in the on position. This should be evaluated thoroughly. Holster modification or a different holster may be required.

Professional fitting of the thumb safety is absolutely mandatory. The engagement of the safety and the sear must be perfect if you want it to indeed act as a safety and not as an accident waiting to happen.

Ejectors and Ejection Ports

An extended ejector will help ensure positive ejection of the spent cases, as does lowering and opening the ejection port. Professional installation and milling machine skills are required to complete these modifications properly. Installing an extended ejector without opening the ejection port to the correct dimension can create difficulty in ejecting complete cartridges. In the unlikely event of having a failure to fire due to a bad primer or other cause, the complete cartridge will have to be extracted and ejected from the gun to chamber a fresh round. With the extended ejector in place, if the ejection port is not milled to the correct dimensions, there won't be enough clearance to eject a complete cartridge. This can cause a binding of the gun in a critical situation.

Unloading live cartridges from the chamber can also be difficult when using an extended ejector and an ejection port that is not milled to the proper dimensions. These factors combined with an improper unloading technique can cause a live cartridge to ignite when the primer impacts the ejector as the slide is pulled to the rear. This often occurs when the loaded cartridge is too long to escape the port and becomes lodged between the front of the ejection port on the slide and the frame mounted ejector. An ignited cartridge could result in substantial injury to the operator's hand, face, and eyes if he is positioned to take the effect of the blast. (When an unsupported brass cartridge case ignites, it usually fragments and drives splinters of hot brass through the surrounding area. Safety glasses are, of course, mandatory.) Cheap ejectors can break off the extended nose and render the pistol inoperable.

Triggers

A trigger job is another option that is included on most basic reliability packages for the 1911. A quality trigger job does not make the pistol any more mechanically accurate, but it does assist the shooter in using the mechanical accuracy the pistol is capable of. A 1911 can have its trigger pull weight adjusted from very light to very heavy, depending on the shooter's requirements. Mass-produced pistols usually show little attention to the quality of the trigger pull and are delivered with a substantial amount of trigger creep and grit. A trigger job for a defensive pistol should have a proper let off, but not be overly light. A close-range confrontation can be a very physical event, where too light of a trigger can be an unnecessary hindrance. A professional trigger job in the five- to seven-pound range for a defensive 1911 will provide a very long lasting (lasts for many thousands of rounds without needing a tune up), safe trigger pull.

A shooter seeking trigger pull adjustment on a 1911 should not be locked into a magic number of trigger pull pounds, and a shooter who believes that he can only shoot quickly and accurately with a light trigger pull is likely to experience poor performance. Trigger pull management is a skill acquired through dedicated practice. The 1911's trigger pull advantage comes from its short, crisp, consistent pull, not necessarily a light pull. The ultra-light trigger pulls of competition pistols offer only a small speed advantage when getting into high levels of electronically timed competition, a speed advantage too small to be realistic for the defensive shooter, especially when realizing that a stouter trigger return spring resets the trigger more quickly and reliably. A defensive encounter could very likely happen where multiple people grapple for a pistol. Too light of a trigger pull allows for a very slim margin of operator error in these types of confrontations. Shooter experience, however, will be a factor in determining what weight of trigger pull serves the operator best.

There are many new products on the 1911 custom market relating to improving trigger pull. Some of these hammer/sear arrangements are superior for a long-term, reliable trigger job, but others are suitable for competition only. Titanium hammer components have become a fad in the competition circuit as the lighter weight hammers are said to decrease lock time and assist the shooter in delivering more accurate shots. While in theory this sounds logical, in my experience the titanium components have not demonstrated long-term durability. Top quality steel components have proven to be best for a defensive handgun.

Magazine Wells

A basic reliability package on a 1911 also commonly includes funneling of the magazine well. Obviously, this makes insertion of the magazines faster, easier, snag free, and generally more positive. While this modification doesn't necessarily add to the weapon's reliability, it can enhance the shooter's performance, especially if the shooter locks up under high stress and has difficulty correcting the mistake. Snagging the lip of a magazine on a square mag well can slow reloading, and high stress can make correcting the problem difficult. Fine motor skills have a way of deteriorating under pressure.

Feed Ramps and Barrels

Polishing the feed ramp and throating the barrel are two mandatory modifications for better reliability. Throating is once again a job for the professional 1911 pistolsmith, as improper throating can contribute to unreliability, ruin your barrel, and create an extremely dangerous situation when firing the pistol. (Pistols that are factory throated can be very rough.) Also, you should discuss the ammunition you intend to shoot with your pistolsmith before having these modifications completed. Most likely your experienced pistolsmith will have some bullet shape recommendations. A properly throated pistol will give you trouble-free functioning with any reasonably designed bullet shape. Improper ramp work on the frame can also be ruinous.

Polishing the feed ramp and throating the barrel are two modifications that are very often done improperly by persons inexperienced with the 1911 design. The over-throated barrel is not only unreliable, but can allow the unsupported case to rupture and blow out and downward into the magazine well area. This will often blow the stocks off the pistol frame and blow the magazine out of the well. In a worst-case scenario, this rupture could ignite the additional rounds contained in the magazine, making injury to the shooter probable.

Recoil Springs and Shock Buffs

Correct spring weights should also be furnished with a basic 1911 reliability package. The spring rates should be compatible with the ammunition to be used. Consultation is again necessary between the owner and the pistolsmith to determine what ammunition and what spring rate are best. This will allow the owner to be aware of what spring rate is required for spring replacement maintenance. The ammunition type will, of course, also have an effect on the zeroing of the pistol. Selecting light-loaded ammunition for use in a pistol that has springs that are too heavy will result in malfunctions. Using full-powered ammunition in a pistol that contains springs that are too light will cause pistol battering. Correct spring rate selection and installation of a shock buff will minimize such problems.

Shock buffs are rubber washers originally developed by Wilson's Gun Shop and designed to cushion the impact of the slide on the frame. Spring and shock buff replacement should be done at the pistolsmith's recommended intervals. The shock buff needs to be replaced whenever it shows signs of becoming cut. Failure to do so will allow the shock buff to separate and become entangled in the recoil spring. A shock buff must be properly maintained or not used at all.

I don't recommend a shock buff in the Commander model, as it will shorten the already shorter slide stroke even more, which will cause an even choppier slide stroke. The correct spring rate used in the compact Officers model without a shock buff is fine. Properly maintained shock buffs are recommended for high-volume shooting with the Government model.

Extractors

Polishing and adjusting the extractor is another mandatory basic modification for 1911 reliability. Again, there seems to be a problem with mass-produced pistols simply having parts put in place without the proper hand fitting. They commonly come from the factory with rough and improperly adjusted extractors, which can cause a multitude of problems.

The extractor is a key point in 1911 reliability and should never be abused. It is not a pivoting extractor, which means the operator should never drop single rounds directly into the chamber and shut the slide over the cartridge. This can break, damage, or otherwise adversely affect the adjustment of the extractor. Extraction is, however, very reliable when the extractor is properly tuned. A quality extractor very rarely fails unless abused. Always load the chamber via the magazine.

Firing Pin Springs

A more powerful firing pin spring is recommended, especially in pistols of a pre-Series 80 design. Pre-Series 80 pistols do not have the firing pin lock feature of the Series 80 pistols and have the potential of firing if they are dropped and the muzzle directly impacts a hard surface. The beefed-up firing pin spring substantially decreases the likelihood of the inertia firing pin striking the primer when the pistol is dropped and also returns the firing pin into the firing pin stop quicker, resulting in a decreased likelihood that a loose firing pin stop will dislodge from the slide. For this reason, the beefed-up firing pin spring is also recommended in Series 80 pistols. A loose firing pin stop is easily rectified, but if the stop becomes loose under field conditions the spring will help reduce the possibility of a firing pin stop drop malfunction.

I recommend replacing the recoil spring in a Government model at least every 2,000 rounds, the Commander's springs at least every 1,000 rounds, and Officers model springs every 500 rounds.

Barrel Bushings

A solid barrel bushing should be included in every basic 1911 reliability package. It is very important to eliminate the old style of collet barrel bushings, as they have a tendency to break. The collet barrel bushings have flexible fingers that ride on the barrel as the slide moves back and forth. On numerous occasions one or more of the flexible fingers have broken and become lodged between the barrel and the inside of the slide during operation. This results in a complicated stoppage. It is best to eliminate the possibility of such a problem before it occurs by properly installing a quality solid barrel bushing.

Inspection

An overall fit and function inspection should be included, even with the most basic of 1911 reliability packages. Quality control standards have deteriorated in many of today's mass-production businesses and it shows in the products they are turning out.

It is commonplace to locate several minor staking and fitting problems in today's mass-produced handguns as they come out of the box. Correcting these problems is normally not a major project, but left uncorrected will surely result in a future malfunction. Proper fitting or staking of these pins should be a basic reliability package requirement.

Of special interest on the 1911 is the plunger tube housing. For some unknown reason, this particular part is left improperly staked to the frame on a regular basis. I have had numerous 1911-style pistols delivered new from the distributor where the plunger tube housings could be removed with mere finger pressure. In some cases the pistol is equipped with stocks that support and hold the plunger tube housing against the frame, while other stocks offer no support to the housing at all. If this particular item is left uncorrected it can not only interfere with slide stop operation, but can lock the safety in the on position. If the rear of the plunger tube housing comes loose from the side of the frame, the safety lock plunger can easily spring past the safety and lodge underneath the safety's thumb shelf. Once in this condition, the safety will not be allowed to move downward until the safety lock plunger is manually pushed back into the plunger tube housing. This is another problem that should be corrected before it occurs.

Test Firing

A reputable 1911 enhancement service will make it a policy to thoroughly test fire all completed pistols to check for final function, point of impact, and accuracy. This is normally done after discussing the customer's ammunition selection and using the customer's preferred choice of ammunition. Service centers that do not take this final step in assuring proper function will usually have to deal with clientele who are irritated about having to return the pistol for a minor adjustment. A thorough test firing of the completed pistol eliminates the vast majority of these problems.

Upon receipt of the customized handgun, the owner should, of course, complete his or her own thorough test firing of the pistol to ensure proper function with his or her particular ammunition selection and magazines. This test should consist of a minimum of 500 rounds of the particular ammunition used with dedicated carry magazines. It is also the final responsibility of a defensive pistol owner to determine if the point-of-aim and point-of-impact are correct for the operator.

ADDITIONAL MODIFICATIONS

The aforementioned items should be the minimum you consider having done to a 1911 prior to carrying it as a defensive sidearm. There are, however, additional very desirable options beyond the basic reliability modifications that will allow the pistol to handle better and increase its mechanical accuracy, as well as increase the controllability of the pistol. A step-by-step discussion of these modifications will hopefully assist the reader in deciding which options might benefit him or her.

The Beavertail Grip Safety

Beavertail grip safeties are highly recommended and believed by many to be absolutely essential on the 1911. I concur that the beavertail grip safety is a required element for a fast-handling 1911.

There are many manufacturers and designs of beavertail grip safeties. Beavertails, as with all other 1911 options, have been under a constant state of development for many years. Recent developments in these safeties have allowed the shooter to acquire a very high hold on the pistol, which reduces muzzle flip. A few of the most popular designs are the S&A, Wilson, and Brown.

All of these high sweep designs require radius milling of the frame's rear. This is a good idea anyway, because it gives the smith the opportunity to break all of the sharp edges in the grip area. A properly dehorned gripping surface area is very desirable on a pistol that will be repeatedly handled at high speed.

For most hammer designs, the beavertail that mounts high into the frame and allows the shooter to get into more of a direct line with the bore requires a clearance cut by dishing out the top portion of the grip safety, which allows the rear of the hammer to enter the top of the grip safety during the hammer cocking cycle. When the pistol is carried cocked and locked and the hammer is contained within the beavertail recess, it minimizes the chance of clothing being caught around the back of the hammer, which is a very desirable feature. The beavertail also eliminates the painful hammer bite many shooters receive when using a standard grip safety/hammer design.

The high-sweep beavertail grip safety can present an occasional problem for some shooters when disengaging the grip safety following the draw. The correction to this problem was once accomplished by welding a ridge on the bottom edge of the grip safety to allow for more positive depression. New designs incorporate this ridge, also known as a speed bump, into the grip safety's design. Pinning or otherwise deactivating the grip safety, or any other safety device, is not a modification a reputable pistolsmith will make.

The improved beavertail grip safety also spreads recoil over a larger area of the hand, resulting in less felt recoil and therefore faster controlled shooting.

Note: A Commander-style or bobbed Government hammer can be used in conjunction with a high-sweep beavertail grip safety.

There are numerous drop-in beavertail grip safeties on the market that are so poorly designed that they aren't worth installing. A properly designed beavertail should have an upswept tail that allows the shooter's hand to slide into firing position. It should also be capable of being mated with the frame and achieving a fine line fit with no sharp edges. Beavertail grip safeties that leave a gap between the frame and the safety are an open invitation to snagging the web of one's hand. Grip safeties sporting a downward angle on the exposed rear portion are not only more difficult to draw with but force the shooter's hold to be lower on the frame, which translates into more muzzle flip.

The Browning Hi-Power also poses some hammer-bite problems for some shooters, and the short tang on the frame is very snag prone during a draw that is even slightly out of place. Also, the grip safety is not a feature on the Hi-Power, so its takes substantial steps to cure this problem. Another beavertail-like piece can be welded onto and blended into the Hi-Power frame to eliminate hammer bite, and once completed the feature looks original. The sweep angle on the Hi-Power can be adjusted depending on the type of hammer used. If a spurless hammer is used, the upward angle of the fabricated beavertail can be substantial and very comfortable. If a spurred hammer is used, the fabricated beavertail will have to be positioned more straight out from the rear of the frame. For shooters who prefer the Hi-Power design, the fabricated beavertail is a very worthwhile option.

Hammers

Hammer selection is very important for a defensive firearm, but some of the newly designed hammers are only suited for competition use. Ultra-lightweight titanium hammers are not recommended for use on a defensive pistol because their longevity has not been as good as that of quality steel. EDM (electro-discharge machine) cut, tool-grade steel has proven to be a very worthwhile investment for an operator desiring a hammer/sear combination with proven longevity.

Hammers and sears with less-than-reliable engagement surfaces are unwise. The proper hammer/sear combination can achieve a solid, smooth engagement for the defensive handgun without unnecessarily minimizing the contact between the two parts.

A safe and reliable pistol must be maintained as the top priority when selecting parts, and your hammer selection must also be compatible with your beavertail selection. In some cases, full width hammers will not properly enter the dished-out portion of the beavertail. The width of the hammer should obviously be less than the width of the dished-out portion of the beavertail. It is also important that the hammer be functional and not bind in the dish of the beavertail, whether the beavertail is at rest or not. It is also very important that the hammer and hammer strut not be impeded by the intersurfaces of the beavertail, which can obviously create difficulty in operation.

Triggers

A variety of triggers and trigger styles have also become available. Some of these triggers are obviously meant for competition use only, so it is critical that your pistolsmith knows you want a pistol for defensive purposes and has enough experience to know what custom parts are compatible with a defensive pistol as opposed to a competition pistol.

Short triggers, long triggers, extra-long triggers, and pivoting triggers are all available for the 1911. Pivoting triggers shouldn't be considered for use in a defensive 1911, because it is common for glove material to stop a pivoting trigger from being pulled because of the material being wedged between the bottom of the trigger and the trigger guard.

Trigger length is primarily a matter of shooter preference. Shooters who prefer to use only the first pad of their trigger finger, or shooters who have very small hands, often choose a short trigger. I have found that the vast majority of shooters prefer what is known as the standard long trigger, which seems to best suit the reach of most shooters' trigger fingers. The extra-long trigger is used less often than the short and standard long trigger, but is sometimes selected by those who prefer a more extended trigger finger position when shooting. It should also be noted than an extra-long trigger may interfere with a gloved trigger finger's safely entering the trigger guard.

Aluminum triggers are preferred because they are durable and reduce the problem of trigger bounce. Ultra-lightweight triggers, commonly made from skeletonized fiber or with reduced bows, are not recommended because of field durability problems.

Trigger-stop set screws are commonly found in aftermarket custom triggers. These stops can be quite functional and enhance the felt pull of the trigger stroke, but here's a serious word of caution in the area of trigger stops for the defensive handgunner: they must be properly adjusted by a professional to ensure proper function and then be securely set in place. A trigger stop not properly set in place can stop the pistol from firing if the adjustment changes. Therefore, a trigger stop should be properly set in place or not used at all.

Do not attempt to overset a trigger stop on a defensive pistol because it may prevent the pistol from operating properly. An improperly set trigger stop can affect the operation of the safety linkage in a Series 80 pistol, too. (When a trigger is called adjustable, people often think that the adjustment is for pull weight, which it isn't.) It is important for a pistol owner to realize that it is an overtravel adjustment that shouldn't be altered once properly set.

Trigger shoes shouldn't even be a consideration on a defensive pistol because of the high probability of the shoe coming loose and locking the trigger into an inoperable position.

Guide Rods

The use of full-length guide rods in a 1911 is frequently a subject of debate. People who have been thoroughly trained and who are in the habit of doing the old-style pinch check—with the thumb in the front of the trigger guard and the index finger of the weak hand on the front of the spring plug—typically don't like the full-length guide rods because they make the old-style pinch check impossible.

There are substantial benefits to using a properly fitted one-piece guide rod in a defensive pistol including:

- the pistol runs more smoothly and consistently
- the pistol retains a snug fit longer
- the accidental ejection of a chambered round is prevented when the front underside of the slide is impacted.

These features can be taken advantage of and a condition check of the pistol's chamber can still be completed with a modified press check.

A modified chamber check is actually more positive than the old-style pinch check and is easily completed by inserting the thumb of the weak hand in the front of the trigger guard and wrapping all four fingers over the top of the slide in front of the ejection port. This allows for substantial control of the pistol when the slide is squeezed partially open to view the chamber. Front slide serrations assist the shooter even more. A full-length guide rod does not interfere in any way when checking your chamber's condition in this manner.

Another version of the chamber check, which I do not feel is as stable as wrapping four fingers over the slide, would be to grasp the sides of the slide in front of the ejection port from underneath the frame

The solid one-piece guide rod offers a number of advantages.

with the thumb and forefingers. While the check can be performed this way, it is not as stable as the previously described method.

The benefits of full-length guide rods are several. The slide is centered in the frame during operation and runs smoothly on the guide rod, the function of the pistol is smoother, and a slide guided by the rod puts less uneven stress on the frame rails. This translates into a pistol that will remain snug between the slide and the frame longer.

One function the guide rod provides, which is overlooked by many shooters, is the fact that the slide cannot be pushed back to the point of ejecting the chambered round from the front underside of the slide. This feature is very important because a five-inch Government model without such a rod can have the front underside of the slide pushed back far enough to eject the live round from the chamber. If the slide is not pushed fully to the rear, the live round will be ejected but the slide could close before picking up the next round in the magazine. This, of course, would leave the shooter with an empty chamber. I learned of this problem in a live-fire incident where the front of the pistol was brought over a solid cover object and the front underside of the slide impacted the cover. I was staying as low as possible in order to use the cover well. When the front underside of the slide impacted the cover

A chamber-checking port milled into the barrel hood to allow a quick visual check of the chamber.

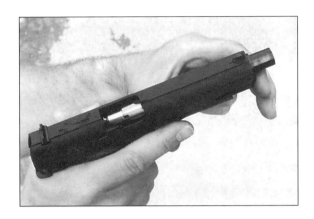

The four-finger daylight check, pinch check, underside slide check, and night check. All are quick and easy.

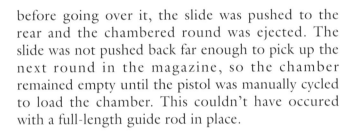

before going over it, the slide was pushed to the rear and the chambered round was ejected. The slide was not pushed back far enough to pick up the next round in the magazine, so the chamber remained empty until the pistol was manually cycled to load the chamber. This couldn't have occured with a full-length guide rod in place.

Chamber Checking

When considering methods of chamber checking, especially in live encounters where maintaining a firing grip on the pistol is desirable, one may want to evaluate milling a small observation window in the barrel hood. In fair to good lighting conditions, this will allow the operator to merely glance at the barrel hood and determine if there is brass in the chamber. This is a very effective, quick, and silent method of chamber checking.

In poor light conditions, however, the chamber will still have to be checked by feel. This is easily accomplished by wrapping four fingers over the top of the slide and holding the thumb and the palm tightly against the slide opposite the ejection port. The slide is retracted slightly and the index finger on the left hand (when shooting right-handed) is inserted into the slide just behind the barrel chamber area. The cartridge will be semi-extracted from the chamber when the slide is moved to the rear and the index finger can feel whether the round is in place. Index finger pressure should be directed inward rather than downward to ensure the operator doesn't dislodge a loaded round from the breach face/extractor. Once confirmation of a round being in place is made, the slide can be released forward and the thumb safety engaged. Do not cover yourself with the muzzle when performing these maneuvers.

Grip Surfaces

An improved grip surface is also highly desirable. Most beginner shooters don't realize the benefits of an improved grip surface until they have acquired and established their particular shooting grip style. Once this is achieved, the shooter will be able to realize the importance of proper grip control on the pistol, especially during rapid fire. An improved grip surface is a very important feature, particularly when the pistol is to be handled in all climate conditions, with gloves or sweaty hands, under rapid fire, or under dirty or wet conditions.

Improving your pistol's grip surface is best accomplished with metal checkering, although there are less expensive methods of improvement, such as stippling or friction tape. However, friction tape rarely stands up to extended use. (General use and cleaning are often enough to make friction tape peel off of a well-used gun. Repeated applications of friction tape will be required to maintain its grip surface and oftentimes results in sticky glue residue being left behind.)

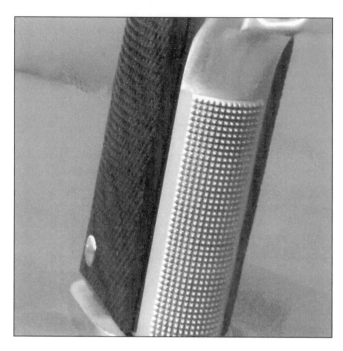

Hand-cut checkering. Buyer beware: inexperienced attempts at checkering metal can ruin the looks and resale value of your gun.

Stippling of the grip surface on a 1911 is desirable by some shooters, but the grip surface provided by stippling is not as positive as that from checkering.

Most people consider checkering more attractive cosmetically and more effective grip-wise than stippling. The drawback to hand-cut checkering is the cost. Some machine-cut checkering is nearly as expensive and rarely has the cosmetic appearance or grip surface of professionally hand-pointed checkering. This is an area each individual shooter will have to evaluate and decide upon on their own.

I don't recommend the stamped sheet metal aftermarket checkered strips that are held in place on the 1911's front strap by the stock panels. These sheet metal strips have been known to slide down the front strap and interfere with seating the magazine.

A cautionary note on 1911 metal work should be observed. Improperly completed metal work on the 1911, or any other firearm, is not only ineffective, but can be a terrible cosmetic problem. This obviously reduces the resale value of your pistol. Inexperienced attempts at customizing 1911s have ruined many quality firearms.

Wraparound rubber grips are a less expensive alternative to a metal checkering package, but aren't nearly as effective. Rubber grips give you a fatter grip area, a spongy feeling, and are slippery when wet. Rubberized recoil-absorbing grips may be a consideration for a hard-recoiling magnum revolver, but on the moderately recoiling autopistol they are not needed. Thus, most experienced shooters shy away from wraparound rubber grips. A good set of hardwood stocks combined with a metal checkering package will give the shooter a thin, fast-handling grip frame area with enough traction for good control during rapid fire.

Trigger Guards

Hooked and squared trigger guards used to be popular modifications on 1911s, but because of the development and refinement of most experienced shooters' shooting styles, these modifications have become less popular. Many shooters have found that the index finger of the support hand wedged underneath the trigger guard can not only assist in aligning the sights on the gun, but can help the shooter avoid dipping the muzzle during the trigger break. I have found that wedging the support-hand index finger under the trigger guard allows for the most secure hold. Simple serrations on the front of the trigger guard allow for added grip surface in this area when the index finger of the support hand may wind up there during a fast draw. These serrations allow the shooter to secure the weak-hand index finger on the front of the trigger guard and accomplish the shot without wasting time repositioning the weak-hand index finger. Horizontal serrations on the front of the trigger guard have proven to work better than checkering in this area because the support-hand index finger often slides in from the side and attempts to negate upward muzzle flip. Vertical serrations on the trigger guard to finish a checkered pattern simply cause the support-hand index finger to skid rather than slide into place.

It is not uncommon for some 1911s to have a trigger guard that is too thin to deeply checker without welding additional thickness to the guard. Avoidance of welding to the frame is desirable whenever possible. In some cases, the trigger guard thickness may be such that it requires finer serrations, as coarse serrations would cut too deeply into the guard.

I don't recommend checkering or serrating underneath the trigger guard because this is an area where the fingers need to be allowed to slide into a firm wedged grip. The underside of the trigger guard and the area at the top of the front strap and the rear of the trigger guard should be left smooth and free of any sharp edges. A properly checkered or stippled front strap will then allow the hands to be held high in this area in conjunction with the high-sweep beavertail. This high hold will place the shooter's grip nearly in line with the bore. This, as I mentioned earlier, is desirable for controlling muzzle flip during rapid fire.

Typically, the two mainspring housing shapes that are available for the 1911 are flat and arched. Recently, Ed Brown Custom Products produced a new style of mainspring housing. This housing is marketed as the "wedge" and, in my opinion, is very effective at furthering the shooter's ability to retain a high hold on the pistol during rapid fire. Conversely, the flat mainspring housing doesn't give the bottom of the shooter's strong hand any stopping point to hold the hand high on the grip, and the arched mainspring housing hits in a less comfortable area of the palm of the shooting hand for many operators. The new Ed Brown wedge, when dehorned, is quite comfortable for most shooters and greatly assists the shooter in maintaining a high grip. It is available in a plain surface model, which allows the pistolsmith to finish it to match surface improvements used elsewhere on the pistol. I have found that a slightly less aggressive texture or checkering may be desirable on the wedge. Metal checkering in the area of 30 lines per inch works very well with this housing because the angle of the housing provides some support by protruding out and away from the bottom rear of the grip frame. Twenty-lines-per-inch checkering on this protruding mainspring housing has been determined to be a little too coarse for many shooters' hands.

Slide Serrations

Serrations on the rear of the slide are not there, as many people seem to think, for you to slam your hand against during a feedway malfunction. You certainly can slam your hand against them, but if your pistol is having feeding problems, get the problems corrected and save your hand. The hand-slam method of malfunction clearance is far from the best technique, as we will see later. The serrations are designed to shadow out any glare coming off of the rear of the slide when shooting with your back to the sun or bright lights. As Hollywood as it may sound, obtaining a position with the sun at your back is a wise maneuver in a defensive encounter.

The serrations on the rear of the slide are also designed to blend in with the serrations you have on the rear blade of your rear sight. This allows the entire sighting area on the rear of the pistol to look the same, which reduces the chances of a distraction taking your concentration off the proper focus on the front sight. Also, the blending of the serrations on the rear of the sight with the serrations on the rear of the slide is cosmetically appealing. Nonserrated rear sights usually have other features that allow the rear sight notch to be distinctive and shadow out glare without the need for serrations. These types of sights often feature a recess notch that provides for a no-glare sight picture.

Cosmetically, nonserrated sights look best when blended with nonserrated slides. Sights such as the low-mounted Fixed Novak and the low-mounted adjustable MMC are cosmetically appealing when they are blended into the lines of the slide. The rear slide surface is then matte finished to reduce reflection.

A serrated slide top may be effective in reducing reflection and glare off the top of the slide, but in reality, if the pistol is at eye level and the sights are aligned, the top of the slide is not visible. In most cases, a serrated slide top is simply a matter of cosmetics. Slide top serrations should be approached with caution, because if the slide top requires flattening before serrating, it can be dangerously reduced in thickness in the area of the locking lug recesses. If slide top glare is a concern, a less expensive but just as effective result can be acquired from matte finishing the slide top.

Magazines

Quality magazines are crucial. Magazine problems have been one of the reasons that shooters interested in the ultimate in reliability have come back from the double-column auto to the single stack. Quality single-stack magazines are superbly reliable and maintainable, whereas double-stack magazines can cause a variety of problems, especially when dirty. A thoroughly trained shooter can reload in one second, and a moderately trained shooter can easily accomplish the task in approximately two seconds. With this reloading speed possible and considering the cost and subsequent ban on high-cap mags, the

Much thought and testing have to go into selecting extended extra-capacity magazines.

high-capacity magazine becomes less of a consideration. There is nothing wrong with a higher-capacity auto, provided it doesn't adversely affect reliability, concealability, or handling. If it does, it should not be considered for a defensive pistol—and it often does. High-cap pistols can be used very effectively by disciplined shooters, but the defensive shooter must ensure that he doesn't fall prey to the spray-and-pray mentality often generated by high-capacity weapons. Moreover, some high-cap pistols have become so large as to be impractical as concealable defensive sidearms. (Trying to design the pistol into a primarily offensive weapon has simply resulted in an oversized and awkward handgun. If a compact, pistol-caliber weapon is sought to be effective between pistol and carbine distances, a HKPDW-style unit is more practical. However, this direction in weapon development is away from the compact, daily carried defensive sidearm.)

The only magazine I currently recommend for defensive 1911 use is the Wilson seven-round Number 47 stainless steel magazine, which has proven itself reliable through hundreds of thousands of rounds and is maintainable by simple parts replacement.

The reason the seven-round Wilson magazine is recommended over the eight-round magazine is, again, consistency as well as reliability. A fully loaded seven-round magazine seats into the autopistol with approximately the same amount of force whether the slide is open or closed. A fully loaded eight-round magazine can require a substantial impact on its base pad to seat it when the slide is closed, but the same magazine will seat easily when the slide is locked to the rear. During high-speed reloads, which might be done with the slide locked open or closed, seating will need to be consistent to ensure proper "felt" feedback.

The seven-round magazine features a two-legged convex or rounded-top follower, which keeps the cartridges at the proper angle for feeding (this is true from the first to the last shot). The follower then provides positive last-shot lock-open operation on pistols that incorporate that feature.

During hard use, magazines with welded base plates can fracture and result in the magazine spring and cartridges shooting out of the bottom of the magazine. Once this happens to a welded baseplate magazine, it is often considered scrap. The Wilson magazine may occasionally break a base pad, but normally it cracks before separating completely. Routine maintenance procedures and inspection of the base pads on your pistol's magazine will allow you to detect any developing cracks and replace same for a minor expenditure. Even if the base pad were to completely fracture and fall off of the magazine, the retaining plate, which is contained inside the inwardly curved bottom lips of the magazine, will hold the spring and rounds in place, thus allowing the pistol to function. Routine maintenance and not dropping magazines onto hard surfaces provides substantial magazine longevity.

Magazine springs are another critical element. To allow rapid fire, the column of cartridges must be snapped into feeding position smartly. Cartridge delivery is where the single stack has an advantage over the double. Double-stack magazines commonly roll the cartridges against each other and the sides of the magazine, whereas single-stack magazines simply shove a straight line column up into feeding position. Dirt or sand can quickly stop many doubles, while the single stacks continue to function.

I recommend that the springs be replaced every three months in magazines that are always kept loaded. Spring life can be increased further by rotating and resting magazine springs on a routine basis. While magazine springs may be capable of lasting much longer than my recommendation, on a defensive pistol, reliability has to remain your primary concern. Vendors who say their springs don't weaken and never need replacement are simply salesmen.

Routine cleaning of W-R magazines is easy. They disassemble and reassemble easily to guarantee that there is no dirt buildup, which could affect the follower's operation. Replace the spring correctly.

Other magazines with short followers or split-lip followers often fail to keep the cartridge column at the proper angle for reliable feeding, and they fail to get proper last-shot slide lock. Magazines with poorly designed followers can also allow the magazine follower to slip past the slide lock and allow the slide to close on an empty chamber. This is true even in pistols with the last-shot-lock feature fully operational. This could create a consistency problem for a shooter who is used to the slide locking open when his pistol is empty. When this problem occurs, the magazine often fails to drop free. The pistol should always operate one way or the other when it comes to last shot lock.

Various thicknesses of base pads are available for the W-R magazine to suit the various needs of the shooter. Double-thick mag pads are available for use with some magazine wells, standard thickness base pads are available for general carry, and ultra-thin base pads are available for extreme concealment. To compromise between durability and concealability, I recommend the standard base pad.

A note on loading your autopistol magazines: hold the magazine in your weak hand and push down on the top round (or the magazine follower if the magazine is empty) with the weak-hand index finger before pushing in the next round. This relieves stress on the magazine lips, which you should check thoroughly for cracks during routine maintenance. (I have never observed a W-R magazine crack, which I can't say about poor quality magazines.)

W-R magazines are now available for the Colt Officers model and are recommended for use therein. The six-round version with the dual long-leg follower is preferred.

Magazine Releases

I generally do not recommend extended magazine releases because of the possibility of unintentional release. Extended magazine release buttons are quite prone to accidental depression and partial magazine release when the pistol is carried close or tight to the body. The enlarged paddle-type releases are not recommended because they can be accidentally depressed while firing with both hands.

Should your magazine button be pushed while the pistol is holstered or being carried tight against the body, the magazine will most likely only pop out of the gun approximately one-eight of an inch. When the shooter draws the weapon, the magazine could fall out of the gun at that point, or the tension of the magazine release spring may hold the magazine in the partially ejected position. This would allow the pistol to fire the chambered round, but probably not allow the next round to be cycled into the chamber, thus requiring a tap-and-rack stoppage clearance drill to correct. On some occasions, the round in the chamber may fire and the ensuing recoil may cause the magazine to drop past the magazine catch and onto the ground.

Extended magazine release buttons also give the shooter a different feel when releasing the magazine. A pistol without an extended magazine release button has to be slightly turned in the shooter's hand to be depressed. This is true for all but the largest of hands. An autopistol equipped with an extended magazine release button usually requires very little if any shift of the pistol in the hand. A shooter should become accustomed to one and only one type of release to ensure consistency in the field.

A slightly extended magazine button does enable most shooters to eject a spent magazine more quickly, which can minimize shifting of the pistol in the hand and assist in a quicker reload. Should a shooter consider having a moderately extended and sized magazine button installed on a defensive auto, he or she must be sure that the magazine button is contoured to the point that it will not allow for accidental magazine release when using a two-handed grip. Even more importantly, the shooter must be positive that his or her method of carry will not interfere with the extended magazine button and cause the button to be unintentionally depressed. (The inside-the-waistband carry, with or without a holster, should not be considered if an extended magazine release button is on the pistol.) A properly designed holster, which is substantially relieved in the magazine button area, may allow for carrying a defensive pistol with a slightly enlarged magazine button. It is critical that this area be thoroughly evaluated before street carry. In gun-grab situations, the extended release makes unintentional release a good possibility if multiple hands are on the pistol.

Magazine Wells

To be used on a defensive pistol, a one-piece magazine well must be extremely durable and rigid in its mounting to the pistol's frame. Magazine wells that are one piece with the mainspring housing and properly fitted and blended can achieve the desired result. Improper fit of a one-piece magazine well/mainspring housing can cause a binding of the magazine in the pistol's frame, preventing it from dropping free. Provided these units are properly installed, they have proven to be a rugged, reliable, and trouble-free setup. There are many other magazine well designs on the market, some of which use the grip screw bushings and stock panels to hold them in place. Should the pistol be dropped or severely jolted, this style of well could become misaligned and prevent the magazine from being readily inserted or ejected.

Once a one-piece magazine well/mainspring housing is properly blended and fitted, it would take an impact severe enough to actually bend the pistol's frame to cause misalignment. At this point, the pistol's functioning would be doubtful anyway.

There are a multitude of other magazine well add-ons that report an increase in reloading speed. Many of these cheap, aftermarket items are mere plastic add-on devices that certainly won't withstand the rigors of long-term field use.

For reliability, magazine wells that attach to the bottom of the mainspring housing by means of a single socket-head screw still need blending. Marketing this type of quick on, quick off magazine well funnel by saying it can be attached for competition and easily removed for carry will only work well for those who do not put serious thought into the matter. A wise defensive handgunner will maintain the same options on his pistol during practice, competition, and carry, and therefore allow for consistent operation at all times.

Handgun concealment is normally a concern for the defensive handgunner. Adding a magazine well to the butt of your pistol will usually add approximately one-quarter inch in length to the grip frame. In order to ensure proper magazine seating in the pistol, it is commonplace for a shooter to use a magazine with a base pad that protrudes approximately one-quarter inch below the bottom mag well. The combination of an add-on mag well and a magazine base pad that protrudes one-quarter inch below the mag well ends up lengthening the grip frame on the pistol by approximately one-half inch. This should be considered when evaluating the completed pistol's concealability. Some shooters who prefer this type of magazine well will carry a magazine seated in the pistol that is flush with the bottom of the magazine well. This adds a mere one-quarter inch to the bottom of the grip frame. Backup magazines carried on the belt for quick reloading would then have a full-size base pad to ensure proper seating on the reload. This will work well on most occasions, but does allow for a possible magazine mixup or reseating of the magazine with the short base pad following a tactical reload. The most consistency is achieved by using the same magazines and magazine base pads.

Magazine wells are available that require shortening of the grip frame before installation. These magazine wells typically give a substantially larger opening to the bottom of the grip frame while not increasing the overall length of the grip frame area. This design allows for a standard base pad to be used, which in turn allows for excellent concealment while having the advantage of a large magazine well.

The drawback to the older style of magazine wells that were installed after shortening the grip frame was that they often had to be welded or brazed in place. Avoiding welding, brazing, or heating the frame is always desirable.

Richard Heinie has developed an excellent magazine well that eliminates the problems associated with heating the frame. It requires substantial machining procedures to install and can be quite expensive, but once properly installed, it works superbly. The grip frame is shortened and the magazine well is attached in the area where the frame was shortened to ensure no length is added to the grip frame. The magazine well is then held in place by four sturdy screws that are drilled and tapped to the sides of the frame. The rear of the magazine well is contoured to the rear of the grip frame and the inside of the magazine well is blended with the magazine well and mainspring housing. When properly completed, the Heinie magazine well allows for faster reloading without increasing the length of the grip frame. Standard magazine base pads can be used. The durability of this magazine well is superior to that of any other add-on magazine well currently available. (Mag wells that wrap around the front of the front strap can sometimes interfere with the removal of a stuck magazine. This is not the case with the Heinie. A stuck magazine can be removed as easily as if the frame had no magazine well installed.)

Aftermarket extended enlarged magazine wells have been popularized by action pistol competition. The enlarged magazine well provides a substantial advantage in the ultra-quick magazine change. There are several magazine well designs currently available, some of which don't possess the durability required for defensive handgun carry.

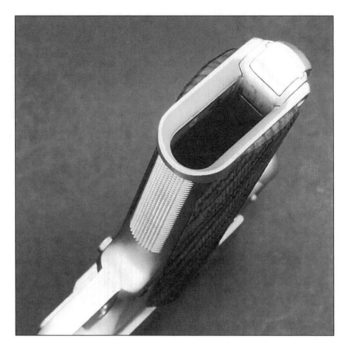

The Heinie mag well.

There are numerous extended magazines available for the single stack 1911 that incorporate a stop on the front rounded surface of the magazine. This type of magazine may not be compatible with magazine wells that extend around the front strap of the pistol. They usually require the bottom of the unaltered front strap to stop them from overseating into the pistol. Overseating the magazine can be a problem, especially when loading the pistol when the slide is locked to the rear. An extended magazine that doesn't have a stop properly engaged at the bottom of the front strap can also cause problems if the shooter is firing prone and the magazine is resting on the ground.

A rigid extended magazine is often used as a monopod in prone competition shooting. If this technique is attempted with an extended magazine that doesn't have a stop rigidly engaged with the bottom of the front strap, the magazine can be seated deeper when the slide moves to the rear, which will stop the forward movement of the slide during return travel. You must consider whether you plan to use extended magazines if you intend to use this style of magazine well.

For the concealed carry defensive shooter, extended magazines probably aren't a desirable option, and for the competition shooter desiring added magazine capacity, a combination mainspring housing/magazine well would work better. My advice to the defensive shooter is to consistently use the same magazine size and capacity.

Choosing a magazine well that is installed after shortening the grip frame will also require inletting of the stocks for proper seating against the frame. When this is done properly, the pistol has an overall excellent professional appearance.

Long-Slide Conversions

Long-slide conversions were popular in the late 1970s, but gave way to compensated autos in the early 1980s. The long-slide conversion has made a comeback in the 1990s because of its allowance in the stock gun class of IPSC shooting. While the recoil dampening advantage has to be given to these compensated autos, the long slide still has its own advantages in that the extra weight does dampen recoil to some extent, and it has an extended sight radius and excellent accuracy when properly fitted.

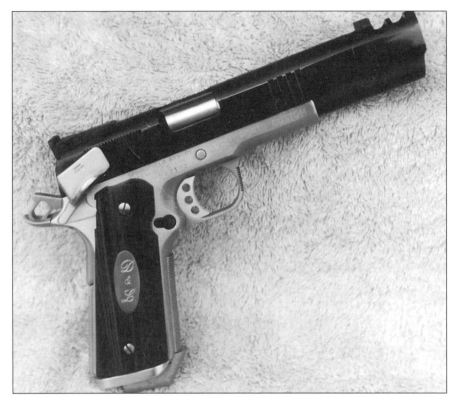

Compensator pistols have substantially reduced muzzle flip.

A custom six-inch long-slide .45 auto.

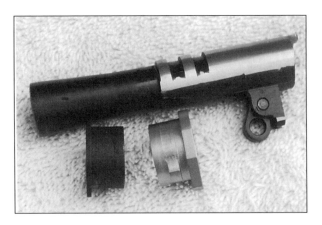

The heavy duty Officers model barrel bushing (right) compared to the standard Officers model barrel bushing (left).

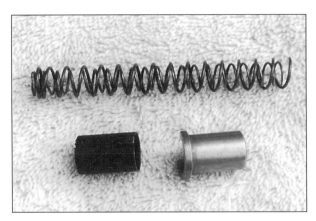

The heavy duty Officers model spring plug (right) compared to the standard Officers model spring plug (left). Note the small retaining tab on the standard plug compared to the thick collar on the reinforced plug.

The long-slide 1911 is considered by most to be on the large side as a concealed-carry defensive pistol, but it can be used as such if the proper concealment holster is used and the slide length doesn't exceed six inches.

While outside of the modifications scope for a defensive pistol, the long-slide auto also makes a good choice for those who want to use a scope. The long slide can be very accurate, and the muzzle blast of the noncompensated long slide doesn't soot up the front lens on the scope.

Those considering a long-slide auto should determine which recoil springs are available. Some pistol salesmen will tell you that a standard five-inch Government model recoil spring and plug will work fine in a six-inch or longer long-slide pistol. Whereas in some cases they may work, they will not work as efficiently as they should. A long-slide conversion should include a custom-made spring plug, which allows the spring to deliver proper operating tension. This means that the front inch of the spring plug should be solid or only allow the guide rod to pass (not the spring) beyond the length of a standard five-inch plug. This allows the operator to select from a variety of available five-inch Government model springs and achieve the proper spring rate and tension for the load he or she is using.

Officers Model Modifications

If you have chosen an Officers model, I highly recommend that a reinforced spring plug be installed. The Officers model barrel bushing/spring plug setup puts all the recoil spring's operating force onto a small tab on the spring plug rather than the barrel bushing. It is common for the retaining tab on the recoil spring plug to shear off, resulting in your plug and recoil spring shooting out the front of the pistol. This, to say the least, is a bad situation. The slide will remain it its rearmost position and the plug and spring will probably be forever lost if shooting under field conditions. In true emergency situations, an operator could manually cycle the next round into the chamber and cause the pistol to fire. This, however, is not recommended unless it is a dire emergency. If it is necessary, remember that the slide must remain in its forward position for the pistol to fire. This position could be easily maintained by light thumb friction on the side of the slide during trigger pull. Again, this is not something that should be practiced, but a defensive shooter should be aware of its potential. The best solution is obviously to cure the problem before it happens.

This weak tab feature came to the attention of the serious shooting field shortly after the Officers model was introduced. Since that time, numerous manufacturers of top quality aftermarket products have introduced items to cure this problem. There are now not only quality reinforced spring plugs available, but spring guide rods and heavy duty barrel bushings as well.

Modern dual recoil springs for the Officers model have also been greatly improved. The properly installed dual spring system for the Officers is now capable of operating smoothly and efficiently. Early problems with the dual spring system kinking together led toward the development of short, stout, single springs. These springs appeared to work better than the original dual spring systems, but they could fatigue and take a set in their compressed position. Although the modern dual spring system has been performing very well, because of the recoil pounding this compact pistol takes, I still recommend replacing the recoil springs every 500 rounds if it is going to be used for a defensive pistol.

Slide Stops

Ambidextrous and extended slide stops are not recommended for defensive pistols because they are highly snag and malfunction prone. The added weight and size of an extended slide stop makes your pistol likely to lock open before it is empty, and such a stop may not properly fit many holsters. Provided proper technique is used, an extended or ambidextrous slide stop is not necessary for the proper operation of a pistol, a fact we will discuss more later.

Cast metal slide stops have proven to be less than durable on a long-term defensive pistol shooting full-power loads. While the inferior part can break in the cross pin area, this is relatively rare. More commonly, the cast slide stop will break the retaining tab that retains the slide stop into the pistol. Once this retaining tab is broken, the slide stop can come out of the pistol's frame without aligning it with the disassembly notch in the slide. Occasionally this tab will be broken by the inexperienced operator attempting to get the slide stop in or out of the frame. Other times, a cast slide stop tab can simply fracture. Quality heat-treated slide stops are now available and are a wise investment for the shooter who wants the most durable and reliable pistol available.

An option that some people prefer is elimination of the last-shot lock-open feature of the 1911. This is an option that requires serious thought before application. Elimination of this feature allows the pistol to be fired dry and after the last shot allows the slide to go forward on an empty chamber. This is a desirable feature for some experienced shooters because it drastically minimizes the possibility of having the pistol falsely lock open when there are still rounds remaining in the magazine. False locking is more of a problem with double-stack magazines in wide-body autos, but can occasionally occur with the single-stack design.

There can be various causes for an autopistol to false lock, but one of the most common is shooter grip interference with the slide stop. During recoil, the shooter can sometimes bump the slide stop into its upward position which, of course, stops the slide in its locked open position. Various bullet shapes can also knock the slide stop up during the feeding cycle. Elimination of the last-shot lock-open feature on the pistol

The 1911 slide stop with retaining tab.

minimizes the possibility of these or other false lock problems. It is a wise option but one reserved for the experienced shooter.

A shooter who feels the need for his pistol to mechanically indicate to him that it is out of ammunition should retain the last-shot lock-open feature. The shooter must also be aware that the locked open pistol is a signal to his adversary that the pistol is probably empty. The shooter whose primary interest is total reliability and who has enough experience to keep the pistol in a loaded condition will enjoy a final edge of added reliability with this option.

On occasion, when a pistol is shot dry because of a mistake or necessity, the use of a magazine with a convex follower, such as the seven-round W-R, sufficiently slows the empty slide's forward movement to avoid lug battering. In the case of shooting the pistol dry and needing to reload, the shooter simply inserts the magazine and racks the slide. In a situation where the shooter is unsure if the chamber remained loaded, a chamber-checking window in the hood of the barrel is helpful. In emergency or dark conditions, the operator simply racks the slide each time a fresh magazine is seated to ensure a loaded chamber uses a night check. The slide stop still maintains its manual operation capability so the pistol can be locked open manually, but it wouldn't have the ability to unexpectedly falsely lock the gun open.

Should this option be chosen, operational technique that is compatible with this feature has to be used. Shooter experience in keeping the pistol loaded without fail will be necessary with this option.

Note: The original H&K MP5 submachine gun developed its reputation for reliability without the last-shot lock-open feature. Simplicity has a substantial amount to do with reliability.

Sights

Many shooters prefer an adjustable sight to allow easy, precise zeroing. While the fixed-sighted auto can be precisely zeroed, it normally requires a milling machine to make professional adjustments for specific loads.

The Bo-Mar adjustable sight has long been favored. The only acceptable installation of a Bo-Mar sight on a defensive autopistol designed for concealed carry would be a low-mount, milled-and-melted installation. This means that the sight is milled deep into the slide and all the relevant sharp edges are dehorned.

The Bo-Mar sight's dovetail can be directly fitted into the slide's standard high 65-degree slot, but it will result in a very snag-prone, sharp-cornered, fragile position. Installing the Bo-Mar in the slide's standard dovetail also requires an excessively high front sight in order to zero the weapon. This setup may be common in bull's-eye shooting competition, but it is unacceptable on a concealed carry handgun. Milling the sight down low into the slide will give it a substantial degree of protection.

The low-mounted Bo-Mar remains fairly snag-free in the low-mounted position, even without the corners rounded. Some shooters prefer the corners to be rounded to eliminate the sharpness, while others like the broad, square sight picture because it helps them avoid canting the pistol when aiming.

I have seen a few Bo-Mar sights fail even when properly mounted on full-power autopistols. In these cases, the rear blade sheared off during recoil on high-mileage pistols. Although these stress fractures were rare occurrences, they did occur. Murphy reminds us that things that can go wrong, will go wrong. In the case of a defensive encounter, things that can go wrong will go wrong at the worst time. Losing the rear blade on your sight during a live encounter is certainly going to make sight alignment more difficult, although it should not take you out of the fight.

The Wichita adjustable sight has been popular on the Gold Cup as a replacement sight, the reason being that the Wichita sight is capable of covering the slot already in the Gold Cup slide, which housed the original fragile factory Ellison sight. In recent years, quality dual-spring leaf sights have become available for the Gold Cup and are a better replacement sight than the Wichita.

The latest entry into the quality adjustable sight field for the 1911 is made by MMC. This is the adjustable sight that I currently recommend. As of this writing, I have installed nearly 200 sets of the relatively new MMC adjustable combat sight and have yet to have a failure of any kind.

The MMC adjustable sight is snag-free, has protective ears, is night-sight-insert compatible, and is fully adjustable. The elevation adjustment is accomplished with a small Allen head screw in the side of the right protective ear. The windage is adjustable in a standard drift manner and it holds its windage setting with a massive locking Allen head set screw.

The MMC sight has the approximate profile of a Novak sight and it is possible to low mount the MMC in a durable, snag-free position.

Many defensive shooters determine what load will best fit their needs, zero the pistol for that load, and stay with it. This allows for consistency between training, match shooting, and street carry. If this is your preference, fixed sights will probably suit your needs. Once a good fixed sight is installed, they are extremely durable.

A variety of custom fixed sights are available for the 1911. Some can be mounted in the high-profile dovetail, which comes standard on the 1911. Other fixed sights require milling into the slide with nearly as much machine work as installing adjustable sights. If a shooter uses a separate competition pistol with Bo-Mar sights installed, fixed sights with a very similar sight picture are available that allow for sight picture consistency between competition and carry.

The most professional installation of fixed sights is the low-mounted, milled-in installation of such sights as the Novak or Heinie. Once installed, these sights are snag-free, provide a good sight picture, and are extremely durable. Fixed sights such as these are preferred.

Ghost ring sights for pistols are becoming more available. Most appear to be high profile gimmicks. However, Gary Paul Johnston has designed a rear sight incorporating the lower half of a ghost ring into a Novak-style sight base. It allows for a U-shaped notch, which allows for more light and observation room on both sides of the front sight.

Calling a set of sights fixed is quite deceiving because they are actually adjustable for point-of-impact with the proper equipment. Consultation between the shooter and the pistolsmith should allow for determination of the shooter's ammunition as well as the sight picture and hold the shooter prefers.

It is also important to determine at what distance the shooter would like his pistol zeroed. Once a zero is established with a full-power defense load, point-of-impact will remain quite close when at close to moderate distances.

I highly recommend the addition of night sight inserts. Older methods of sight alignment under low-light conditions have proven inferior to properly set up night sights. There are a variety available to cover a host of shooter preferences. There are three dot, three dots using two colors, bar dot, and dual bar dot night sights.

The night sight configuration you use will be somewhat dependent upon the regular sights you chose, because some iron sight configurations are incompatible with all night sight installation procedures. The three-dot system has become quite popular when it uses two dots in the rear sight and a different colored front sight dot. The bar dot system is also popular because there is no logical way to mix up rear bars in a front dot. A prospective night sight buyer should consider the fact that the night bar installation is not considered as durable as the dots, hence the bars are not covered by the night sight manufacturer's warranty. This warning may be overly cautious, however, because I have used bar dot night sights for more than 14 years without a single problem.

A common argument presented against night sights is that they might be visible to an opponent in dark conditions. While it is true that night sights are visible at night, it is normally only from the rear of the pistol. Another argument is that if it is too dark to see your sights, it is too dark to be shooting. This is obviously untrue, and anyone experienced in low-light shooting is aware that in many situations you can positively identify your target in low light. The problem occurs when you align your dark-colored sights on a darkly dressed adversary. Whereas the light may be completely sufficient to positively identify

A dual-port carry comp pistol with hard chrome finish.

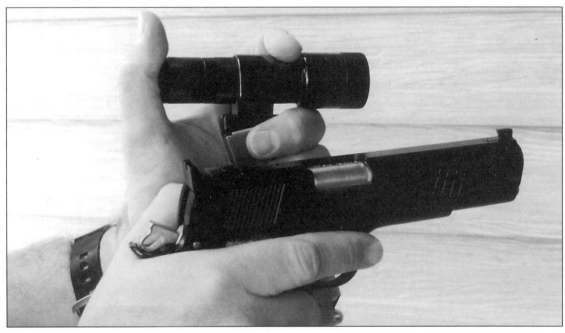

In the event of a tactical reload, the magazine-mounted light can be inverted in the support hand for continued use.

the target, the dark sights get lost against the dark target. Night inserts provide a method of positive sight alignment with dark sights on a dark target.

The old method of firing a round to silhouette your sights in the muzzle flash is obviously unacceptable under most conditions. A defensive shooter should select a cartridge that has a very low muzzle flash, so this particular method of sight alignment in low light would be only moderately effective. Acquiring a sight picture in this manner commonly results in the loss of the sight picture when the pistol is moved, wastes ammunition, gives away your position, and is dangerous.

Once the lighting conditions become so low that positive target identification is no longer possible, a selective auxiliary lighting source becomes mandatory. Options for lighting the defensive pistol are numerous and separate lights are even more available. I have experimented with a variety of lighting techniques and have found that lights mounted alongside or underneath the dust cover of the frame are generally impractical in the field, because you can't immediately reholster the pistol without a special holster, and there is a delay in attaching the light. Also, lights that require wired pressure switches unnecessarily complicate the pistol. Pressure switches often require squeezing to activate and the switch and trigger can be confused under stress. Slide-stop mounts can compromise reliability, too.

Lights that mount over the top of the pistol can not only interfere with reholstering, but also with spent case ejection. I have found the magazine light mount to be the most practical. When properly constructed out of durable (not plastic) materials, the magazine-mounted light is very functional and allows the shooter to light mount his weapon as quickly as he can insert a magazine. No additional wiring or switches are needed if the light integrated into the magazine is a rear-switched durable light, such as the Surefire 6P.

The magazine-mounted light does not interfere with one-handed reholstering when hands-on measures are required, and it can be turned on while the pistol is still holstered, in certain situations. This will immediately put a bright light on the target as fast as the shooter can draw.

A common comment about magazine-mounted lights is that the light will become ineffective once a reload is completed. For tactical officers, a second magazine-mounted light is wise, but for general defensive encounters, expending more than a magazine of ammunition is unlikely. However, if the defensive shooter does complete a tactical reload, all that is necessary to retain his single magazine-mounted light in a functional position is to turn the magazine upside down and operate the light with the weak-hand thumb in a pistol-type grip. This can then be used side-by-side with the handgun to cast effective light on the target.

There are a variety of separate light and handgun techniques, none of which are more effective than (or even equal to) the magazine-mounted light, and none of which allow the shooter to maintain his everyday two-handed solid hold on a pistol. A separate light requires occupation of the support hand. Weak-hand support techniques while holding a flashlight are not as stable as two hands directly on the pistol.

For shooters opting for the separate light and handgun low-light technique, I have found the side-by-side method more desirable than the crossover style. Surefire's small combat light is conducive to the side-by-side method with a syringe-type (blink on, blink off) activation, which allows for both handgun control and tactical flashlight use. For daily carry when low-light shooting is not generally expected and a magazine-mounted light is not practical, the combat light works well. For night patrol, carrying the lighted magazine in the holstered pistol works very well.

The magazine-mounted flashlight comes into its own when the actual confrontation is in progress. For the tactical or defensive shooter, simply making contact with the suspect doesn't necessarily mean that shots will be fired. This is oftentimes a critical moment in the encounter and will decide if the encounter is going to escalate. Once direct contact is made and stealth is no longer a primary factor, the end cap on the magazine-mounted flashlight can be locked on, allowing the shooter to use both hands in a standard, firm firing grip, which in turn allows for target illumination, target identification, and a means of observing the suspect's actions while remaining fully capable of delivering accurate shots. This allows the shooter to have a comfortable, solid firing grip while issuing commands to the suspect.

The operator who locks a light on must be able to extinguish the light if necessary, even in the event of switch failure. Although I have never experienced switch failure on a Surefire product, the 6P light could be extinguished by unscrewing either end. In a worst-case scenario, a mag-mounted light that won't turn off could be ejected if drawing fire. This is more difficult with a more permanent mount.

Experienced criminals may feign compliance or act as if they are having trouble hearing the commands being given. This may be a tactic to create an opportunity to attack. In either case, the confrontation may be prolonged as the criminal evaluates whether his tactics will be effective. A prolonged confrontation with a separate light source and firearm may prove difficult. Attempting to gain further assistance via radio (or cell phone) while trying to manage a separate light and firearm may prove impossible. A prolonged confrontation using any of the separate light illumination techniques along with the handgun may also prove very tiresome and result in the shooter losing control of the situation. In its locked on position, the magazine-mounted light will allow illumination and handgun coverage of the suspect while allowing the operator to have his other hand free.

When searching with a light-mounted handgun, the shooter should be aware that using the light will direct the pistol at whatever or whoever is illuminated. One must be sure that the situation justifies covering a person or object with a firearm. During tactical patrol procedures in gray areas of searching and locating potential suspects, it is common to use a separate high-intensity light for searching and then switch to the light-mounted handgun if the situation dictates. This technique has proven to be both safe and effective in live encounters because the suspect can be located, illuminated, and observed with the main high-intensity flashlight while the officer acquires cover. The officer can then rotate the end cap of the magazine-mounted flashlight into the locked on position while the pistol is still holstered. The pistol can be drawn and brought to the support hand and then take over target coverage and illumination while the other flashlight is dropped or replaced on the belt. This will put the officer in the position of having a solid two-hand hold on the weapon while not losing sight of the suspect.

Safeties

An ambidextrous safety on the 1911 is another area in need of serious evaluation. As with single-sided extended safeties, an ambidextrous safety can be overly large and snag prone unless the proper safety is selected and correctly contoured to the side of the pistol. An overly large safety, especially an ambidextrous one, can result in it being brushed off while the pistol is carried in the holster or hand.

The left-handed 1911 operator would obviously want a left-handed safety lever. The same left-handed shooter may decide he wants the right-handed safety lever on the ambidextrous safety trimmed down to minimum dimensions. This allows primary operation of the pistol with the stronger left hand and occasional weak-hand operation using the right-hand lever. It is critical that the left-handed shooter have the pistol properly set up for primarily left-handed operation in terms of the installation of a left-handed safety lever. Improper installation of a poor quality ambidextrous safety will result in excessive slack on the side of the left-handed lever. An experienced pistolsmith will use a stop to prevent the downward movement of the left-handed safety lever and to give it a resting point for the shooter who shoots with his thumb on top of the safety. This minimizes the chance of slack developing between the joint of the two safety levers—an occasional problem with ambidextrous safeties. It should also be noted that the detent action on a 1911 safety set up for a left-handed shooter will be less than that of a single-sided safety lever for the right-handed shooter, because the plunger that activates the detent action was primarily designed for the right-handed safety lever. Again, to minimize torque and the possible development of slack on the left-handed safety lever, the detent action may have to be made slightly less positive. This might be cured in the future by the development of a left-handed plunger assembly for the frame of the 1911, but for now the 1911 can be set up properly for the left-handed shooter by an experienced pistolsmith who installs a rigid left-handed safety stop and applies the proper detent action.

In light of the development of 1911 features that allow the pistol to sit extremely deep in the hand, I prefer to no longer use ambidextrous safeties primarily designed for use by the right-handed shooter. The reason being when the pistol is set very deeply in the hand, even a well-contoured left-handed safety lever on an ambidextrous safety can dig into the right-handed shooters inner knuckle in its high position on the frame. This is typically not a problem for low volume shooters, but when practice and training are taken seriously, the inside knuckle area of the right hand may become quite irritated. Also, the left-handed side of the ambidextrous safety is required to slide between the shooter's high grip and the frame when it is disengaged. Even a well-contoured left-handed safety lever area makes the shooter aware of this sliding action when the safety is disengaged. If this distraction and the irritation to the shooter's hand can be eliminated, the shooter can shoot with a more positive high grip.

Shooting with a right-handed high grip on the pistol using the thumb on top of the safety hold with a single, strong-side safety lever allows the shooter to shoot at high speed with no grip interference and no occasional maintenance on the left-handed safety lever. It can be made to engage and disengage with a positive detent action, which allows the pistol to be carried concealed close to the body without substantial concern that the safety will be accidentally brushed off.

To be prepared for an incident that may require left-handed shooting, left-handed shooting techniques must be mastered by the right-handed shooter who uses a single-sided safety. This is still quite possible with the single-sided safety. Its positive detent action allows the shooter to fire left-handed without requiring that he hold the left-handed safety lever in the down position for fear of reengaging the safety during recoil. This would be a concern with a safety lever that did not feature positive detent action.

Disengaging the safety lever on the left-handed draw or during any left-handed acquisition of the pistol is no problem for the trained and practiced shooter. In some cases, the safety can be disengaged as the pistol is transferred from the right hand to the left hand. In the event that the strong hand is disabled and the pistol needs to be drawn or the safety disengaged with the weak hand, both can be easily accomplished. Once the pistol is acquired with the left hand, should the safety lever be engaged and there is a need is for the safety lever to be disengaged, the shooter can simply move his left-hand thumb to the safety lever side of the pistol and disengage the safety before repositioning his thumb into a firing grip on the pistol's frame. Obviously, the finger would not be on the trigger during this maneuver.

Some shooters with the dexterity to do so will use the rear portion of the left-hand trigger finger to disengage the standard strong-side safety as needed.

If the pistol is acquired from the ground or other location, the safety position needed can be determined at the time the pistol is acquired and placed into the correct position while the gun is still in contact with the supportive surface. With proper practice, these will all become simple and effective methods of using a 1911 left-handed with a strong-side-only thumb safety. (Practice should obviously be completed in a safe, building-block manner until the shooter becomes adequately familiar with the techniques.)

Model 1911 shooters who use the thumb-on-top-of-the-safety-lever technique have several advantages in defensive encounters. A shooter who is well trained in this technique will be able to acquire a firing grip and draw the pistol into the developing situation without deactivating the manual thumb safety, which will stay on until the instant before firing is required. This adds an additional measure of safety to the encounter, not to mention providing a potentially successful gun snatcher with an additional obstacle. Users of this technique will know that depression of the safety will require no additional time in getting rounds down range. Firing with the thumb on top of the safety also ensures that the safety is not accidentally engaged during the firing process. When the shooter has completed his firing sequence, the safety returns to its on position and the thumb returns to its position on top of the safety. This allows the shooter to draw, disengage, shoot, reengage, and move or otherwise continue the encounter with a manually activated safety, making possible an extremely fast-handling handgun with a manual safety that can be activated in all encounters where firing is not in progress. The 1911 is truly a superior design in this area.

Shooters who prefer to shoot with their thumbs underneath the safety will have a delay from the time they disengage the manual safety and reposition their thumbs under the safety into their preferred firing grip. To avoid any delay in the time it takes to fire the weapon, shooters who use this technique are more apt to disengage the safety earlier than necessary. This negates the safety lock obstacle for the successful gun grabber and is not recommended. The low thumb hold also allows for the possibility of bumping the safety back on during firing and causing a stoppage.

The technique a shooter develops in regard to thumb positioning on the safety is directly related to training and experience, and shooting with the thumb on top of the safety is certainly the preferred technique. As related to disarming techniques, neither hold is superior to the other in terms of grip on the weapon. This high-thumb technique does make it more probable that the safety will be in its on position during a potential fight for the gun.

To effectively use the high-thumb technique, a beavertail grip safety with a positive engagement ridge at the bottom edge is recommended. This technique can sometimes open the palm area of the hand and not allow for proper depression of the grip safety. The grip safety with the raised ridge, also known as the speed bump, allows positive depression of the safety, even when using the high thumb hold.

Another area that may be of concern to some shooters when using the high thumb hold is the possibility of friction being applied along the sides of the slide during slide reciprocation. When the thumb is maintained in position on top of the extended safety lever, some shooters' thumbs can come in contact with the slide, which can translate into slide retardation and incomplete operation if thumb-to-slide contact is substantially tight.

To eliminate this possibility, some shooters prefer to have a thumb guard installed on the pistol, which places a barrier between the thumb and the slide. The thumb guard should be rigidly mounted to the frame and allow complete unrestricted slide reciprocation without exerting any pressure on the slide. Also, a thumb guard will partially or completely block the rear slide cocking serrations, so slide activation from the rear cocking serrations will be difficult or no longer possible. This is a desirable feature when considering gun grabbers. The trained shooter will be operating the slide from the front serrations. The successful gun snatcher may be confused by his inability to retract the slide from the rear serrations, which allows another time delay for the defensive shooter to employ countermeasures. (More on this later.)

To eliminate the need for a thumb guard, some shooters use a manual thumb safety with a low lever, which allows the shooter to maintain thumb position on top of the safety while not interfering with the slide's operation. While this seems like a logical solution, many shooters find the different feel of the low safety lever to be not as comfortable as a standard high-extended lever.

There are several thumb guards available. I recommend a rigid frame-mounted thumb guard rather than a budget, thin sheet metal thumb guard. The stocks will have to be inletted for use with a thumb guard to achieve proper fit. Interchanging stocks from that point will not be possible without inletting additional stock panels. As with other options for the 1911, professional installation of a quality thumb guard is required.

Enlarged thumb safeties that incorporate an integral thumb shield have proven to be a poor choice for the defensive handgun. Conversely, the frame-mounted thumb guard has proven to be more durable and more compact for serious field use and carry.

Accurizing the 1911 for defensive handgun use is recommended, although this has long been viewed as an area that will cause unreliability. (Loose and sloppily fitted handguns have always been touted as being more reliable.) While improper accuracy work (most lousy work, for that matter) can cause unreliability, a knowledgeable 1911 specialty pistolsmith can provide services which will make your 1911 not only superbly accurate, but more reliable than any sloppily fitted autopistol.

The key to reliability is proper modification and consistent operation. As an additional benefit, the consistently operating pistol provides much improved accuracy. In the case of the properly tuned 1911, a knowledgeable pistolsmith can obtain both reliability and accuracy. Cosmetic appeal is a third obtainable goal in modern professional pistolsmithing.

SHOOTING UP TO YOUR PISTOL

Accuracy enhancement work is recommended for shooters with the skills to take advantage of it, along with beginning shooters willing to make the commitment toward being good marksmen. However, a fully accurized pistol will only shoot as good as the shooter and ammunition. A new shooter shouldn't expect to be able to buy accurate shooting skills by purchasing an expensive pistol. Shooting skills have to be practiced and perfected through dedicated training and practice. On the other hand, the new shooter should also keep in mind that an inaccurate pistol can add frustration to his new shooting career by falsely leading him to believe that his shooting skills are not improving with dedicated practice. For example, an inexperienced shooter who has a pistol capable of shooting one-inch groups at 25 yards, and who is only capable of shooting 10-inch groups at 25 yards, will shoot approximately 10-inch groups at 25 yards, leaving much room for improvement. The shooter's goal should be becoming capable of shooting near the mechanical accuracy of his pistol.

A shooter who has a pistol that is mechanically capable of shooting 10-inch groups at 25 yards and who is personally capable of shooting approximately 10-inch groups could be shooting in the area of 20-inch groups at 25 yards. At best, the shooter would only be capable of improving his group pattern down to approximately 10 inches with the best of personal skills.

I prefer an accurized pistol precisely sighted in for my shooting style. This allows me to know that a missed shot was most likely human error, requiring me to go back and hone my basic shooting skills rather than blame the inaccuracy on the pistol.

Many 1911 pistolsmiths offer basic and deluxe accuracy work. Basic accuracy work often includes standard reliability work, plus snugging the slide-to-frame fit and properly installing a match-grade barrel bushing. Both of these items can be completed without adversely affecting reliability, provided they are done correctly, and they will improve accuracy.

Barrels

A deluxe accuracy job often includes basic reliability and accuracy work, plus the installation of a premium match-grade barrel. There are obviously various types of match-grade barrels for different cartridges operating at different pressure levels, but whereas integral feed ramp barrels may be required to achieve proper cartridge case support in high-pressure cartridges, the standard .45 ACP 1911 is best served with a standard ramp match-grade barrel.

Contrary to what has been written about 1911 match barrel installation, a match barrel can actually increase reliability as well as accuracy. I have developed specific procedures for this area to ensure reliability. Fitting procedures are critical. A misfit 1911 barrel can cause a multitude of reliability problems. The drop-in barrels commonly installed in mass-produced 1911s are sometimes so poorly fit that they adversely affect reliability and accuracy. A knowledgeable pistolsmith can fit an oversized match barrel to the dimensions of the individual pistol. When people request the utmost in reliability, whether they have a concern for increasing accuracy or not, I highly recommend a properly installed match-grade barrel.

Nevertheless, improper installation of a match or standard barrel has the potential for disaster. You must ensure that an experienced, knowledgeable pistolsmith knows that your 1911 is to be suitable for duty use and not competition use only, because the tolerances will be different in the two fitting procedures. In my opinion, an accurate pistol that is unreliable is totally unacceptable.

When selecting a match-grade barrel for use in a noncompensated 1911, I recommend a barrel and bushing set of near-standard configuration rather than a cone barrel system, which eliminates the barrel bushing, because a bushingless cone-to-slide lockup allows for extra movement of the muzzle end of the barrel when the slide is in its rear position picking up the next cartridge from the magazine. Without proper support, the cone barrel system can allow the barrel throat area to tip up and cause feeding problems, and it also exposes more of the pistol's internal workings when the slide is out of battery.

With no barrel bushing around the outer diameter of the barrel, more contaminants are allowed into the area between the slide and the barrel. Even if this does not produce a stoppage, it certainly can produce more slide-to-barrel wear by grinding grit between the two surfaces.

Another critical factor that must be considered with both comp guns and cone barrels, which incorporate a flange attached to the end of the barrel, is the possibility of debris becoming lodged between the front of the slide and the rear of the compensator or flange and stopping the pistol from going into battery. This is a serious concern when shooting prone in a dirty environment, or during contact shooting where clothing may be caught between the front of the slide and the rear of the compensator or flange. This will, of course, stop the operation of the pistol. A standard barrel and bushing setup, on the other hand, will minimize debris from getting between the slide and the barrel in the first place, and it will commonly push off other items that may come in contact with the barrel by the forward motion of the slide and bushing.

Recoil reduction attained with a noncompensated cone barrel verses a standard barrel and bushing setup is indistinguishable to many experienced shooters. Claims of dramatic recoil reduction of cone over conventional barrels is simply salesman talk.

Compensator systems for the 1911 have developed substantially since the 1980s. The goal of these systems was to reduce muzzle flip and increase accurate shooting speed. More recently, compensator development has continued to allow for rapid, accurate shot delivery while reducing felt recoil and not interfering with the optical sight picture, which has become popular in modern competition shooting.

Compensator systems range from very effective and quite expensive to drop-in add-on weight kits. Some companies even market slotted extended barrel bushings billed as compensators. The area of recoil compensators for the 1911 is not only a buyer-beware market in terms of quality, but also in terms of effectiveness.

Drop-in barrels are obviously not going to give you the match accuracy of a properly fitted match barrel and may suffer from serious reliability problems. Normally, the cheap alternative to a properly designed compensator body is a small weight silver-soldered onto a drop-in barrel.

Debates often arise over which compensator system is best, including whether the conical barrel lockup or the barrel bushing system is more effective. The cone barrel compensator system typically employs a 1911-style barrel with a conical sleeve, a one-piece conical barrel, or a taper-turned comp back. The cone system eliminates the barrel bushing and locks up directly between the front end of the slide and the conical portion of the barrel, which has proven effective in competition but still suffers from the aforementioned problems.

The bushing-style comp system uses a standard diameter match-grade barrel and a quality bushing system. The barrel normally extends beyond the bushing for comp attachment via machine-cut threads. Quality systems of either style perform well in competition circles, but further consideration must be given to each system by the shooter to determine what options will suit him best.

A quality compensator system costs substantially more than the aftermarket drop-in comp kits, but the resulting accuracy and reliability are worth the expense. Many pistolsmiths specialize in guns only for competition, so if you are considering a compensated carry/combat pistol, you must be sure your pistolsmith is knowledgeable in the field of comp guns designed for defensive purposes. (There are substantial differences in pistols set up for defensive purposes and game guns.) Comp guns have obtained the undeserved reputation of being game guns. A properly designed comp on a match barrel installed on a combat weapon will not adversely affect reliability under normal conditions, and will enhance rapid fire controllability. Additionally, a properly designed and fitted compensator on a combat pistol will give the shooter increased sight radius, added muzzle weight, an effective expansion chamber for reduced recoil, and the mechanical ability to place superfast follow-up shots with excellent accuracy.

Once a new shooter progresses past the stage of point-the-pistol-and-jerk-the-trigger and starts aligning the sights for each shot, no matter how fast, he or she will see a benefit in a quality compensator system. The practical combat competition arena has shown the compensator to be both reliable and practical for increasing shot-to-shot speed with full-power ammunition.

A word of caution: I am aware of only a few pistolsmiths producing compensator combat pistols. The trend of building carry comp pistols has been increasing, but make sure you are not delivered a pistol set up for competition instead of rugged duty. Many competition-only pistolsmiths do not consider the possibility of the pistol's reliability being a life and death factor.

The drawback to carrying a 1911 with a compensator as a defensive pistol are considered substantial by some. A few factors to be considered are:

- A compensator added to the end of a standard pistol will increase the pistol's overall length.
- Having a 1911 slide cut back to allow for installation of a compensator without affecting the overall length can cause function problems under certain conditions.
- A conical lock-up compensator system exposes more of the internal workings of the pistol to the environment.
- Anytime a muzzle-end attachment is installed on a defensive pistol, one must remember that the pistol can be stopped if foreign matter comes between the front of the slide and the rear of the muzzle attachment; this can be a difficult stoppage to clear rapidly in field conditions.
- A compensator-equipped pistol will typically be more complicated to disassemble and maintain on a daily carry basis.
- A compensator-equipped pistol may require the use of a specially designed holster for daily carry.
- Increased low-light muzzle flash is more common on a comp gun.

In light of newly developed products for the 1911 that allow for a very high, comfortable, and firm grip by the experienced shooter, many have found that muzzle control on the modern noncompensated defensive auto is nearly equal to rapid fire control experienced with the originally developed compensator pistols. The addition of new grip enhancements to the 1911, in addition to a compensator system, will be even more effective in the recoil control department, but will still add the complications of the compensator system to a daily carry pistol. Many experienced and knowledgeable modern defensive shooters have gone back to the noncompensated, single-stack, customized five-inch 1911 as their all-around carry pistol, and can now compete on an even playing field in pistol matches, such as the Single Stack Classic. The simplicity, reliability, and long-term durability of the properly modified single-stack pistol has been proven time and time again. (The FBI's Hostage Rescue Team members have long carried the single-action autopistol. This choice obviously has a lot to do with performance. The HRT recently made the switch from the single-action Browning Hi-Power to the 1911. The features requested on the HRT pistol are along the same lines as those requested by experienced practical 1911 shooters.)

Magazine Capacity

The issue of magazine capacity has been an influencing factor in the development of the modern 1911. Whereas I believe there is nothing wrong with increasing magazine capacity, as long as it does not adversely affect reliability and create other problems, in some cases the double-column magazine in the widebody 1911s has not proven field reliable. The wide-grip frame has been objectionable because of its inherent handling characteristics. Retaining the widebody frame and its poor handling characteristics, while only using magazines with a 10-round capacity (because of recent magazine-capacity legislation) defeats the widebody's purpose. Some shooters overlook the poorer handling characteristics of the widebody frame to acquire the higher magazine capacity. The single-stack .45 ACP is fully capable of using 10-round magazines that protrude from the bottom of the pistol without the wide grip.

The cost of pre-ban high-capacity magazines is another consideration. Since the magazine capacity rules came into effect, some pre-ban high-capacity 1911 magazines have been selling for $100 or more. This may be acceptable to some, provided long-term durability could always be ensured, but it can not. Problems with the double-stack magazines have been a recurring issue and the ease with which magazines can be damaged or lost under field conditions is substantial. When they evaluate the problems with other available systems, many people come back to the single-stack 1911 in its classic custom configuration.

The Custom Order

A shooter should thoroughly think out the number and type of options he wishes to have on his combat autopistol, realistically considering what will best suit his needs. If the shooter is on a limited budget, he should evaluate which options will serve him most effectively, especially in the reliability department. Once a shooter has decided on all the modifications he needs, I recommend having them performed all at the same time and applying a quality final finish at the end. Whereas this may be a larger expense incurred at one time, it will be a less expensive procedure in the long run. Returning your already finished pistol to your pistolsmith for additional options can become very costly because of the finish needing to be stripped and reapplied and the sights reinstalled. In the event that night inserts were installed and the sights have to be removed, you will most likely need a new front sight and night insert because of the installation procedure that is required to attach the sight. It is simply best to do the job right the first time.

Many pistolsmiths require a partial down payment when your order is placed. This gives the client time to acquire additional funds for the final payment. The turnaround time will vary from smith to smith and from season to season, and a final bill is normally delivered when the pistol is nearing completion. Doing business with a smith that gives personal and professional service in a friendly, helpful atmosphere allows you not only to decide which options will best fit your needs, but also allows you to work out payment arrangements to have all the work done properly at one time.

The cost of what has been commonly referred to as a "full house" custom 1911 can give those not familiar with the custom pistol field the same effect as sticker shock on a new automobile. The costs of the best aftermarket parts used by a reputable smith are substantial. Labor time and the detail work necessary to complete a professional-grade 1911 is such that most smiths don't even want to know what their per-hour rate works out to be. All things considered, the components, time, and craftsmanship that go into a full house autopistol, and the performance that it is capable of, make it well worth the cost.

Finishes

A final finish will have to be selected as a protective coating and it should be selected as carefully as all of the other options. Bluing looks nice when it is new, but it has little resistance to holster wear and rust-causing climatic conditions. Two-tone pistols with bluing and hard chrome are very attractive, but the shooter has the same wear problems with the blued half. Also, one must consider that rebluing the slide on a 1911 equipped with night inserts will require removing and later reinstalling the sights and inserts. This is normally no problem with the rear sight and inserts, but the front sight will usually require a new insert and front sight because of the installation procedures involved in front sight attachment.

Parkerizing has wear characteristics similar to bluing and is not a very attractive finish, and gold, silver, and nickel plating are not recommended for the carry pistol because of durability problems. Show guns look fine with the fancy plating, but it is a waste of money on a practical carry pistol. There are a multitude of new-wave finishes available. Many of these finishes are here today, gone tomorrow affairs that never establish a dedicated following.

For those who absolutely require a dark-finished handgun, the Teflon coating currently available

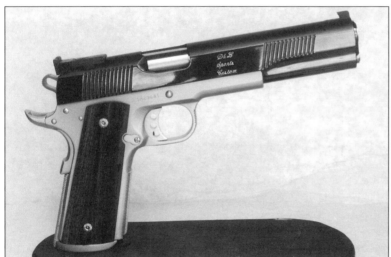

A 1911 with a polished blue slide and satin hard chrome frame (left) compared to a gloss black Teflon finish over hard chrome.

has proven to be superior to most other dark finishes. Teflon can be applied in a variety of ways and colors, including black, tan, green, and various camouflage patterns such as desert, woodland, and tiger stripe. I recommend silver hard chrome (black hard chrome isn't durable), which is available in a variety of appearances, including nonglare matte, a brushed stainless steel, and a mirror polish. Matte hard chrome is a no nonsense, flat gray color similar to gunboat gray. This finish is quite durable and certainly nonreflective, and aside from the cosmetic appearance, it has another benefit: it won't wear off the pistol. However, it can take on a shine when repeatedly drawn from a snug holster. (The holster will certainly not wear through the finish, but you may get shiny streaks on the matte hard chrome in areas where the pistol is in contact with the holster. This is only a cosmetic consideration and not a durability problem.)

The mirror hard chrome is just as the name implies, as brightly finished as a mirror. This particular finish is only applicable to certain handguns, as it requires substantial surface preparation to apply. Some

A black finish over hard chrome is a good choice for the tactical operator.

handguns that are rough on the surface or that have shallow engraving will not be good candidates for this fancy finish. Practically speaking, the defensive handgunner probably won't want such a highly reflective surface on his autopistol because it can be a problem in low light conditions.

For years I have recommended the brushed hard chrome finish, which is very similar to that of brushed stainless steel. The flats of the pistol are often lightly brushed to the point of looking like stainless steel, and the rounds of the pistol, especially the slide top, are finished in a satin matte surface to avoid any reflection. A brushed hard chrome pistol features all the durability of hard chrome as well as long-term good looks. Properly applied, the hard chrome finish will not crack, chip, or peel. I have had hard chrome pistols in service for more than 20 years without requiring refinishing. Hard chrome is extremely resistant to adverse weather conditions and makes routine maintenance quite easy.

I cannot recommend any other finish more highly than hard chrome, but I have used a two-layer handgun finish similar to that used on the D & L professional grade precision rifles. This finish is for those who want a black pistol surface and white hard chrome durability. A matte hard chrome finish is applied and an overfinish of black Teflon follows. This dual finish continues to provide metal protection even when some areas of the black finish become worn. The drawbacks are that it is twice the cost of a single finish and the outer black surface eventually wears and shows the underfinish. This is not a problem on working pistols but is a cosmetic consideration.

Base handgun selection is very important. Selection of a stainless steel autopistol is not normally recommended. In the event a stainless steel autopistol is all that is available for customization, the work can be completed followed by a hard chrome overfinish, which eliminates the galling problems

All of the modifications you choose must be functional under all conditions.

associated with a snug fit stainless steel autopistol. The hard chrome finish will also increase surface longevity of alloy pistol frames, but does require a nickel undercoat to adhear, and nickel can occasionally peel. Overall, blue steel, rather than stainless steel or alloy, is the best base pistol material. The most popular Series 80 Colt five-inch pistols I recommend as base pistols are all available in blued steel: the Colt Government, enhanced Government, and 1911A1. (The enhanced version has the factory undercut trigger guard and a higher price tag.)

Finally, a new, unfired pistol is best to submit for customization. If a factory defect that cannot be corrected is located, it is easier to obtain a replacement for an unfired pistol.

Chapter 4

HOLSTER SELECTION

Disarm the people—that is the best and most effective way to enslave them.

—James Madison

When in a fight to the death, one wants to employ his weapons to the utmost. To die with one's sword still sheathed is indeed most regrettable.

—Miyamoto Musashi
Japan, 1700 A.D.

This chapter will focus on concealed street carry for the defensive handgunner.

A wise shooter doesn't put substantial thought and expense into customizing a superior defensive handgun and then carry the pistol in a poorly designed holster, because the handgun will not be practical as a defensive sidearm if it can't be quickly presented. Making the right selection the first time will give the shooter a system he can spend time practicing with and therefore become proficient with, rather than being concerned about constantly upgrading his equipment to something he should have bought the first time. Although purchasing a practical quality holster and related accessories along with a custom defensive handgun can add up to a substantial investment, like a quality pistol, a quality holster will probably last you a lifetime. There should be no compromise in quality when selecting your carry holster and accessories.

HOLSTER CONSIDERATIONS

The environment in which the shooter will operate will have a bearing on the type of holster that will best suit him. For example, a military-style flap holster offers good handgun protection from the elements, but is slow on presentation. However, when the handgun is carried in dirty conditions as a secondary backup weapon, a quality flap holster may be an option. Another example are the dedicated speed competition holsters, which have become more and more radical in design over the years. Such holsters may allow for a fast draw in specific competition exercises, but most are impractical for street carry. A defensive shooter who is going to carry a concealed handgun must select a holster that provides a logical balance between speed, retention, and concealability.

General Concerns

One of the most important considerations in selecting a carry holster is safety, which not only concerns holding the pistol securely under all conditions, but also includes muzzle direction during carry and on the draw.

If a holster can't be worn as designed and doesn't allow the pistol to be safely drawn from any position, it mustn't be considered. Although covering one's body parts with a loaded pistol is actually more a matter of the shooter's safety habits than a holster problem, some holsters are conducive to bad habits. The horizontal armpit shoulder holster is one example.

A typical horizontal shoulder holster.

Drawing from one of these holsters makes it extremely likely that the shooter will cover his own weak arm if not properly trained, and reholstering presents the same problem. Whereas drawing and reholstering can be safely accomplished, the technique used to do so is often skipped by many shooters who use this type of holster. Having the manual safety on or the finger outside the trigger guard is still no excuse for violating the muzzle direction rule. Also, the horizontal shoulder holster carries the muzzle so that it points back at any support personnel. If the shooter does not react well to high-stress encounters, pulling the pistol from the holster and discharging it to the rear is a possibility regardless of the type of handgun.

Proper drawing and safety techniques are extremely important if you select this style of holster. A shooter who carries a point-and-pull handgun, such as a double-action revolver or Glock, will be especially susceptible to firing when drawing if the finger-off-of-the-trigger rule is not strictly adhered to.

Although it does allow cross draw access from a seated position, such as in an automobile, this holster must be evaluated for overall general carry. Just because these rigs are popular in Hollywood doesn't mean they are street practical. (They tend to flop when running and often require two-hand reholstering.)

An area where cross-body-draw holsters work well is the covert draw. A firing grip can be acquired in many situations without telegraphing the action to less observant people. However, when comparing the draw speeds of a horizontal shoulder holster to that of a quality belt rig, where the hand is not on the pistol, the belt rig is substantially faster nearly every time. This is because the shoulder holster wearer not only has to reach all the way across his body to acquire the pistol, but the pistol is facing 180 degrees away from the target. But, when the hand can covertly acquire a firing grip on the cross-body-holstered pistol, especially when seated, the cross-body draw has the advantage.

Many quality holsters can be used without covering problems, but even they require the shooter to be well trained and follow safety guidelines at all times. The holster should feature a covered trigger

Demonstrating the advantage of a properly adjusted and concealed shoulder holster from the seated position.

guard, and the shooter must remember to keep his finger off of the trigger when drawing and reholstering. Prior to street carry of a holstered handgun, one should have a substantial amount of range training and practice and be able to demonstrate safe proficiency in all areas of handgun manipulation. Adherence to this suggestion will greatly reduce a shooter's chances of injury.

Specialized Holsters

Specialized circumstances may require specialized holsters, such as during deep cover ops. In an occupation where the defensive shooter is often required to allow potential assailants in close while engaging them in a battle of investigative wit and street smarts, special considerations will have to be made. For instance, the defensive shooter might be substantially outnumbered and surrounded before there is any indication of a problem. This could also easily occur in an automobile where the assailant is initially allowed to be seated behind the defensive shooter. Conversational distances would most likely be those encountered. There are times when the defender has to be keenly aware of very subtle indicators that may reveal a setup. These situations are complicated even further because instant firepower must be completely concealed and pass the "accidental" bump check for weapons, or the even more intrusive weapons check by a member of the opposite sex working for the suspect. People who carry weapons know how to spot or check others carrying weapons. Dual vertical shoulder rigs attached together behind the back and to the belt provide a viable concealment system, but they have to be extremely secure, tension-fit holsters to retain the handgun in an unarmed physical encounter, while allowing instant access. (Retention snaps or straps in this particular mode of carry are undesirable.) This system gives the option of quickly acquiring one or both pistols with either hand from various positions, which is a very important consideration when dealing with unsavory characters. The draw stroke that is possible when carrying in this manner can be achieved with very little telegraphing of the movement, which is very important when dealing with subjects who are not going to telegraph their intentions until the moment of truth. Experienced criminals can be very skilled at luring one into a position of disadvantage.

Most shooters don't have the need for this dual rig setup on a daily basis—it is primarily designed for specialized activity—and climate and clothing oftentimes negate its use.

The belt-line cross-draw holster rig is very acceptable for all-around use, with the exception of poor concealability. It is very comfortable, allows for a fast draw from nearly any body position, maintains a safe muzzle direction, and puts the pistol in a position that allows for good retention. (The cross draw discussed here is not the old highway patrolman cross draw on the far offside hip, but more of an appendix position cross draw.) This carry allows the shooter fast, safe access with either hand and puts the pistol in a defendable position. Shooters who have been bent over giving aid to a downed subject when multiple other unknown persons are milling about can attest to feeling uneasy when the pistol is carried in the more conventional side position. When your hands are busy, coverage of the side position pistol becomes more difficult.

The appendix (belt buckle) style cross draw may be an acceptable choice for those who work long hours in a seated position, although low crawling with a front holster or mag pouch can expose the rig to contaminants. Presenting the pistol from the cross draw holster while in a seated position is very safe and fast and works well in automobiles. If concealability is not a requirement for you, a cross-draw holster may be an option. However, the majority of defensive handgunners have concealability requirements that eliminate the conventional belt buckle cross draw from consideration.

A shooter must remember that his strong hand will have to travel at least partially across his body to acquire a firing grip on a cross-draw belt holster or a shoulder holster. In certain situations, body positioning will allow the strong hand to be very close to the firing grip without telegraphing an intention to draw. Under these conditions, the cross draw, or cross-draw shoulder holster, may work well. When drawing from more standard standing-start positions, the strong-side belt holster offers more speed.

I recommend avoiding exotic belt rigs and other poorly designed rigs that require the shooter to move unnaturally to make the draw. One rig that comes to mind is the belt holster worn in the small of the shooter's back, the primary alleged advantage of which is concealability. If it requires a coat or long-tailed shirt to conceal it, you might as well use a quality hip holster and gain additional speed in presentation. A pistol concealed in the small of the back usually requires more attention to keep it concealed and excessive body motion to draw it. In a seated position, it could present problems in acquiring the holstered pistol, and the pistol would often be exposed by a coat with split coat tails. (The chance of the coat or shirt riding up over it in an unnatural position is greater than with a properly designed strong-side rig.) Also, going to the ground on your back with this rig can cause unnecessary injury.

Inside-the-pants holsters are popular with some shooters who need a very concealable rig. The most desirable of the inside-the-pants holsters is probably the strong-side behind-the-hip carry. Cross-draw inside-the-pants rigs can be very uncomfortable when any movement or sitting is required. Likewise, I don't recommend clip-on inside-the-pants holsters that are held in place with a spring steel clip over the belt. During a fast draw they are very likely to come out of the waistline with the pistol.

A side note of interest here. A person in a stressful encounter may reach back and draw his wallet instead of his pistol. Such a person probably changes holster positions frequently and fails to adequately practice with any of them. Be consistent.

A variety of quality, inside-the-pants holsters are available. One of the best in terms of quality and

An inside-the-pants holster with double securing straps.

design is available from Milt Sparks Gun Leather in Boise, Idaho. This holster incorporates heavy leather straps that go around the shooter's belt and snap back to the holster, thereby eliminating the problem of the holster being pulled out of the pants when the pistol is drawn.

Inside-the-pants holsters are available with or without thumb snaps, which hold a retention strap between the hammer and the firing pin. The addition of this safety strap needs to be considered carefully, because disengaging the snap may prove difficult when the holster is held tightly against the shooter's body. Some shooters like the additional security strap when the pistol is carried so close to the body that brushing the safety off is a possibility. However, the chances of brushing the safety off are greatly minimized if the safety is properly radiused and contoured to the side of the pistol and has positive detent action. Inside-the-pants holsters that feature a protective flap between the pistol and the shooter's body, as well as a molded segment that conforms to the safety in the on position, also minimize the chances of the safety being brushed off.

Inside-the-pants holsters are available in standard and rough leather, suede, and a variety of other materials. The roughened suede holsters further reduce the likelihood of the holster being pulled out of the pants. Provided a proper holster selection is made and the securing straps are properly attached to the belt, the chances of pulling the holster out with the pistol are highly unlikely no matter what the outer texture.

A rigid opening at the top of the holster (to keep the holster open after the pistol is drawn) is also desirable and allows the shooter to reholster one-handed. Holsters without this option collapse shut and make reholstering difficult. (The ability to reholster one-handed is vital. In close encounters, your weak arm will often be busy fending off an assailant while your strong arm reholsters. De-escalating from firearm to hands-on control is very likely.)

Many people dislike the inside-the-pants holster because it can be quite uncomfortable (when the shooter wears a tight belt, the pistol can dig into his side rather severely). When the pistol is drawn, even a holster with a reinforced opening at the top can leave the shooter's belt feeling loose.

Drawing a pistol that is holstered very tight to the body can present other problems as well. For instance, getting a good grip on the pistol can be difficult, and occasionally grasping one's shirt in between one's hand and the grip on the pistol can be a problem. Also, an inside-the-pants holster and the behind-the-hip (FBI) cant require the shooter to raise the pistol higher to clear than a more conventional holster would. The FBI cant on the holster also requires the shooter to break a locked wrist to grasp the pistol in a firing grip. Naturally, anything that takes your concentration off of the situation at hand must be avoided. Finally, in hot climates, holster material is also a concern, especially for the inside-the-pants carry. A holster that rots when sweated on or when it gets wet will be a problem.

The Straight-Drop, Strong-Side Belt Holster

I have tried most available holsters and finally decided on the straight-drop, strong-side belt holster because it is the most practical all-around holster in terms of concealment, comfort, speed, security, and safety. The quality, well-designed, straight-drop belt holster features a rigid, secure, weather/perspiration resistant and safe design and an adjustable tensioning device. Plus it allows the shooter to acquire a complete firing grip on the holstered pistol. This should include enough clearance to allow the shooter's strong-hand thumb to be placed over the engaged manual safety and middle finger to be in contact with the underside of the trigger guard. This eliminates any need for shifting the shooter's firing grip once the pistol is drawn and allows for a very fast first shot.

Both the speed of the draw and target acquisition are improved by using a straight-drop holster as compared to a muzzle rear cant.

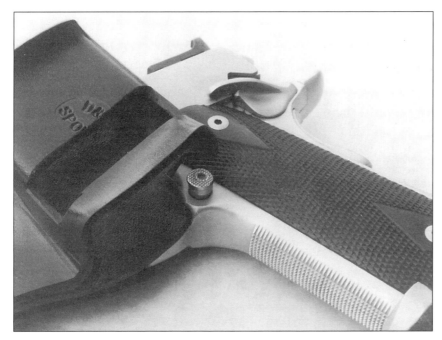
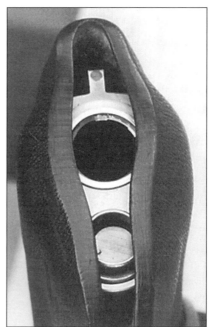

The author's Kydex holster.

I designed such a straight-drop holster—a steel-lined, leather-covered rig produced by Milt Sparks Gun Leather—which has all the desirable features but is quite heavy.

The Safariland Holster Company offers a variety of laminate holsters that feature many desirable traits as well.

I have also designed a general purpose, concealed carry holster for the defensive handgunner made from Wegner Kydex. This material is a PVC and acrylic blend thermally formed to fit the individual pistol. (Kydex is often used in the custom knife field, especially in the area of combat knives, and allows for a very secure carry with immediate and unrestricted access to the knife.) I was able to incorporate the straight-drop holster design features into the Kydex holster, which allows for a straight-drop, strong-side carry that is easily street concealable, very secure, and maintains the speed capability to compete in the best of tactical shooting matches. This makes the "shoot what you carry" principle quite realistic. The holster is tension adjustable and available in the popular straight drop, forward rake, and FBI cant and incorporates an offset in the belt loop design so that the operator can wear a tight belt without causing the pistol to tip inward and dig into his side. The 12-degree offset does not adversely affect concealment and maintains the pistol vertically, which lets the shooter acquire a full firing grip on the holstered pistol and come into a grip position with the strong-hand thumb over the top of the manual safety lever on the 1911.

Once the operator determines the most suitable position for the custom Kydex holster, a slot can be cut in the back of the holster's belt loop for weaving the holster onto the belt. This locks the holster into a rigid position at the correct location for the shooter and therefore eliminates the need for heavy steel-lined or double-thickness gun belts to support a holster on a daily basis when comfort is important. The standard belt loop width is 1 3/4 inches and can accommodate a variety of belts.

A common concern shooters have when carrying a pistol on a daily basis, is weight and comfort. The lightweight yet extremely durable Kydex holster allows the shooter to carry a good steel pistol on a daily basis with no unnecessary weight from the holster.

The Purse Carry

Many women prefer to use a quality purse holster with a handgun concealment compartment, rather than carry the weapon directly on their person. For safety and operational reasons, I don't recommend simply tossing a handgun, especially a cocked and locked auto, into a standard purse. There are several purses available that allow you to attach the purse's carrying strap directly to the handgun inside the concealment compartment. As long as the owner carries the purse by the strap, even if the purse is ripped out of her hands, the concealed pistol will be retained in her hand by the carry strap.

The drawbacks to purse carry are several. Too many women who carry a weapon in their purse don't take it seriously and leave the purse lying around out of reach and unattended. Many children go into purses looking for candy, spare change, and so on, which could result in a serious accident. If you prefer to carry a weapon in your purse rather than on your person, keep the purse with you so the weapon is accessible to you and not children.

A woman who uses a purse carry must also be aware of the pistol's muzzle direction at all times. The purse should maintain the pistol in a single direction so this is possible.

A cocked and locked auto carried in a purse may not be the wisest decision. If there are other items carried along with the cocked and locked auto, a mechanical safety could be brushed to the off position. Firing the weapon from the purse may also be a problem because the exposed hammer might be blocked. Point-and-pull autos with a moderate trigger pull, such as a Glock with a five-pound trigger pull, and an internal striker could lead to an unintentional discharge if carried in a purse and a loose object wedged itself against the trigger.

A dedicated concealed carry compartment and a thorough evaluation of the handgun to be carried is mandatory. A shrouded double-action revolver, such as the Bodyguard or Sentinel, may be the wisest choice for purse carry. If you carry a purse with a strap attached to the handgun, make sure your finger is not in a position to fire the pistol if the purse is snatched. The handgun will remain with you in case the snatcher attempts a personal attack, but, generally, you do not want to shoot a person over a small-time theft, accidentally or otherwise.

Unwise Safety Shortcuts

If you choose a belt holster, you should consider what muzzle angle is right for you. If you follow competition shooting matches, you've probably noticed that most top shooters use a strong-side holster with a muzzle-forward cant and often wear it in front of their strong-side hip for a fast draw from the often used surrender position. But some competition shooters are foolhardy enough to wear the pistol so that it covers their body. A safety violation made to gain additional speed is unwise, to say the least.

You should carry your pistol on duty in the same manner you practice. To do otherwise will result in muscle memory leading you to the wrong position to acquire the pistol in a high-stress encounter, thus delaying the draw when you need it most. This is especially noted when training tactical officers who normally carry a high-ride holster switch to a thigh-mounted holster for tactical training. When they go for the pistol, they grab for the belt line and then have to search down the thigh for the pistol.

Personally, I don't like any carry that puts the muzzle to the rear behind the strong-side hip. This type of carry, while very concealable and comfortable (especially when driving or sitting) creates problems by canting the grip forward, which requires the shooter to break his locked wrist when grasping the pistol. This, in turn, often forces the shooter to lean forward with his upper body, which makes for a slower draw in most circumstances and requires additional movement to get back into a proper shooting stance. Those who have studied martial arts and learned the importance of maintaining a low center of gravity understand the balance problem that can occur when one leans his shoulders forward, especially toward the threat. Using a proper center of gravity stance requires the shooter to have very little shoulder movement and results in a faster draw. Economy of motion will simplify and speed the draw even more. Nevertheless, if the FBI cant works well for you, by all means use it.

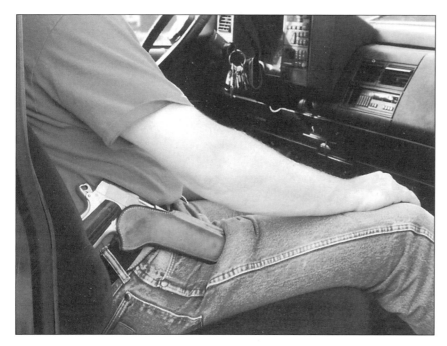

*The Safariland thigh-mounted
tactical holster.*

*In the seated position, the forward-raked holster can point the firearm at the
wearer's body.*

Magazine Pouches and Belts

A quality magazine pouch and belt complement the holster. For general defensive carry purposes, I recommend an open-top, friction-fit magazine pouch. The pouch should feature enough grip on the magazines to retain them under rigorous physical movement, yet still allow a fast magazine draw. A double magazine pouch should be designed to carry the magazines in a single direction, because consistency of the magazine position facilitates consistency during the draw of the magazine and reloading of the pistol. For the right-handed shooter using a strong-side carry holster, the magazine pouch is normally best positioned on the left side of the shooter's body at belt level. In this position the pouch should house the magazines with the bullet noses facing forward. (The precise positioning on the belt will be up to individual shooter preference and concealment requirements.) Carrying the magazines with the bullets facing forward allows the shooter to properly index the magazines into the pistol the same way during every reload.

The belt is also a critical element in supporting the handgun, holster, and magazine pouches. A heavy-duty, double-thickness or steel-lined belt is required to support a heavy carry rig. Without this support, the holster positioning will be variable and prove problematic where consistent draws are concerned. The holster that moves on the belt can also present problems when releasing the pistol from the holster. If heavy-duty carry equipment is used, it should be supported properly with a heavy-duty belt. A heavy-duty rig may still eventually become uncomfortable, resulting in the operator occasionally failing to wear it or developing soreness in the waist/hip area.

New technology allows for carrying the same solid, proven handgun and accessories while eliminating the need for the heavy carry rig. The same advancement in technology allows for extremely secure carry of the pistol and accessories in encounters that may become violent before the pistol or any accessories are called into play.

Patrol and tactical officers have different requirements in weapon and accessory carry than the plainclothes defensive handgunner. An effective method for handgun and accessory carry used during patrol and tactical operations is the standard strong-side pistol carry with multiple spare magazines carried in front of the weak-side hip. The initial magazines should be available from an open top, friction fit pouch, which allows for multiple, quick initial reloads. These can be backed up by additional magazines in secured flap pouches. In a situation requiring expenditure of the initial quick reloads, the empty front magazine pouch can be replenished with the magazines in the secured flap pouches. This method assures the operator that additional secure, uncontaminated magazines will be available if needed. (There is always the potential of losing the magazines from the open-top carrier during strenuous physical activity.) Consideration also needs to be given to magazine contamination during activities such as low crawling or stalking. Magazines carried in the forward front position of the body can fill up with debris during these activities. A contaminated magazine, especially one contaminated with sand, should not be introduced into the pistol if it can be avoided. In such a case, the protected magazines from the flap-secured pouch should be used.

Carry more magazines and ammunition than you expect to need. If some get lost or contaminated, you will have spares, and if you find a way to determine how much ammo is enough, please drop me a line.

The multi-compartment fanny pack has become popular for carry of both a handgun and magazines, as well as small accessories. There are numerous designs with varying degrees of effectiveness, and handgun concealment in a fanny pack ranges from acceptable to blatantly unacceptable. The observer who knows what to look for in a fanny pack, as well as in any concealment method, can often detect when a person is carrying a sizable concealed weapon.

The fanny pack is a viable option for handgun carry in certain circumstances, such as during hot weather when it allows the handgun to be concealed without a jacket or long-tailed shirt. The fanny pack rarely allows as fast a draw as a conventional carry holster, but can blend in well in public.

The type of handgun to be carried must also be considered when using a fanny pack. As with the purse, the shrouded double-action, small frame revolver may be best.

The activity you are engaged in will obviously have a bearing on what type of armament you carry and how you carry it. As the saying goes, there is no pistol too small when it comes to concealed carry, and there is no pistol too large when you actually need it. While this may be somewhat of an exaggeration, if you are going to be operating in an environment that requires a defensive handgun, carry one large enough to be predictably effective. My experience in this area never fails to demonstrate the need for a consistent carry method for a sufficiently powerful defensive handgun.

It seems that in times when you need the weapon the most, you will be armed the least.

Chapter 5

AMMUNITION SELECTION

Arms in the hands of citizens may be used at individual discretion in private self-defense.

—John Adams

To limit the scope of this chapter, we will keep our discussion to ammunition suitable for a 1911 chambered for .45 ACP.

In light of all the ammo manufacturers' and gun writers' claims of spectacular stopping power, ammunition selection can be quite a dilemma. My advice is straight and simple: don't be fooled by the magic bullet claims of exotic, expensive ammunition. Instead, concentrate on shot placement and don't sacrifice reliability for anything.

The number one requirement in a defensive handgun is reliability, of which ammunition is a critical component. This should be your primary concern in selecting the 1911 as your defensive pistol, and you must not allow improper ammunition selection to compromise your weapon's reliability. Fortunately, most modern, commercially produced .45 ACP cartridges offer sufficient accuracy when fired from a properly set up autopistol and work well at typical defensive handgun encounter distances.

THE STANDARD LOAD

I have obtained excellent accuracy and overall performance from the Federal Match 230-grain full metal jacket (FMJ; also known as Federal Gold Medal 230-grain hardball .45 ACP) round. The consistency and reliability of the Federal Match hardball round is excellent.

The drawbacks to selecting Federal Match as a defensive cartridge include the high price tag and, for some people, the FMJ round-nose bullet loading (some people feel the added penetration and limited or nonexistent expansion of this round are drawbacks).

The retail price of the Federal Match 230-grain FMJ is approximately $28.50 per box of 50. While this is certainly not in the realm of overpriced exotic cartridges, it can add up to a substantial amount for the shooter who practices on a regular basis. An optional load that has proven to be quite comparable to Federal Match is the budget line of Federal American Eagle, which Federal offers in a 230-grain FMJ

Shooters without the time, knowledge, or equipment to load their own practice ammunition should acquire their ammo from a reputable manufacturer.

.45 ACP load at a substantially reduced price while retaining quality and reliability. People who choose to use the Federal Match as a carry load will typically train with Federal American Eagle hardball as a practice load. The recoil impulse in the point of impact between the two loads has remained as consistent as possible.

Overpenetration allegations against .45 ACP hardball have been substantially exaggerated. While there certainly have been cases where a round completely penetrated an adult torso, there have also been cases where it hasn't. Many cases have indicated that the human head has the capability of retaining a full power .45 ACP load.

FMJ ammo, even in .45 ACP, has been known to occasionally penetrate a torso and exit with little effect, so it becomes a matter of shot placement. For those operating in conditions where penetration of heavy winter clothing and automobile sheet metal and glass are a concern, the hardball .45 ACP is good. The .45 ACP bullet diameter, of course, starts out at nearly one-half of an inch, making further expansion a questionable necessity. The truth is that the full-powered hardball round possesses enough penetrative power to deal with commonly encountered obstacles without overpenetration, excessive muzzle blast, night flash, or recoil.

Choosing A Load

Handgun training and practice can be acquired using the same or equivalent hardball load that you carry on the street at less expense than some of the more exotic ammunition. This allows for consistency in point-of-aim point-of-impact and recoil impulse—two very important considerations when developing a feel for your handgun's operation.

Should you choose hardball for defense ammo, you must be aware of its pros and cons.

- It can provide desirable penetration in some situations and deliver limited impact in others.
- You must place your shots carefully and be especially aware of your backstop.
- Hardball or military issue "humane" ammo doesn't have the hollow point stigma people like to banter about nowadays.

Typical .45 ACP loads in the 185- to 230-grain area generate a muzzle velocity of less than 1,000 feet per second (fps), but the new "Plus P" loads substantially increase velocity to more than 1,000 fps in an attempt to promote expansion of hollow point bullets, which generally do not expand well under 1,000 fps. Additional design developments now allow hollow point expansion at a fairly reliable rate at velocities under 1,000 fps.

Decisions will have to be made on what type of ammunition performance you require, depending on your operating environment.

The increased velocity of heavy bullets normally translates into increased recoil and muzzle flip, which are drawbacks that can adversely affect rapid, accurate shots, and lighter bullets at higher velocity can have about the same recoil as standard loads with heavy bullets, but have more muzzle blast. Additionally, Plus P loads will slam cycle your 1911 harder than necessary. And, of course, carrying Plus P loads and practicing with lighter ones is unwise, as it will prevent one from developing consistency.

Dangerously overpressured cartridges are another problem and can rupture the cartridge case, leaving the pistol inoperable in a critical situation and possibly severely injuring the shooter.

Given all this, I do not recommend disrupting the excellent compromise of speed, power, and accuracy available from the .45 ACP cartridge by attempting to turn it into a .45 Magnum. If you decide that you want to shoot a magnum, then just purchase one that will operate in the performance arena you were trying to reach by overloading your .45 ACP. But remember, though, that a standard well-placed shot will be more effective than a miss or an edge hit with a magnum load.

Avoiding the higher pressure and higher velocity loads that attempt to acquire bullet expansion will move the defensive shooter into the realm of newly designed bullets designed to obtain expansion at velocities under 1,000 fps. These hollow point bullets are often made with very thin jackets that are serrated for easy expansion. In theory, this idea may sound logical, but under prolonged field conditions it proves problematic. For example, the jacket material can be so light (sometimes made of aluminum) that the bullets can't withstand hitting the feed ramp on a regular basis. A pistol that is carried for duty or defense is oftentimes loaded and unloaded without being fired. Loading and unloading the light-jacketed bullets can severely damage the bullet tips and lead to unreliable feeding, no matter how well the pistol is throated. (No, don't put the damaged bullets at the bottom of the magazine and hope you won't get to them during a shooting, one of the many cop tricks to avoid spending money.) A case in point is the original Winchester Silvertip bullet, which proved to have a problem with the being battered and becoming deformed on the feed ramp.

One might think that a reasonable solution would be to just load the pistol with fresh ammunition and leave it loaded to ensure that the tips do not get damaged, but the pistol's lubricant could affect the primers if this is done. (Even if the pistol is loaded with fresh ammunition, if it is possible for the light-jacketed bullet to occasionally deform on the first feed, that occasion might just arrive

Note the deformed Silvertip cartridge on the right, which was cycled several times and received the damage on the feed ramp, as compared to the new, uncycled cartridge on the left.

sooner than you think.) The bottom line is that bullets that cannot withstand the feeding cycle on a regular basis must not be considered for use.

Another area of concern with light-jacketed, lighter-weight, fast-expanding bullets is that of sufficient penetration. Heavy clothing or an intermediate barrier may absorb substantial energy from the round, limiting the bullet's penetration even more. Large individuals, even though not behind any intermediate barrier, may have sufficient bone and tissue to severely limit penetration, resulting in what appears to be a severe wound, but which in reality is nothing of the sort.

Some manufacturers have retained the heavy copper jacket to withstand feed ramp abuse, choosing to greatly enlarge the bullet's hollow point in hopes of obtaining better expansion. One round that comes to mind is the Speer Lawman 200-grain hollow point. This round is typically loaded hotter than many experienced shooters care to fire in their 1911, noticeably generates more recoil than other standard .45 ACP loads, and is seated deep, in addition to having a short, blunt hollow point. While some 1911 shooters find this round quite satisfactory, logic dictates that the overall dimension of the cartridge could be better to allow for more margin of error during the feeding cycle. Frankly, obtaining as much reliability as is mechanically possible (and then some) must be a concern of every defensive shooter. Using a cartridge with a better design will assist the shooter in achieving this goal. (The Lawman 200-grain hollow point has acquired some catchy names among the gun press, such as the Flying Ashtray, Flying Ashcan, and Flying Cookie Cutter, which can influence impressionable shooters. Using a cartridge because of its name or because it looks mean is stupid, and people who recommend cartridges of questionable design have obviously never been in a toe-to-toe encounter where reliability determined the outcome. The fact of the matter is that the expansion tests I have completed with the 200-grain Lawman jacketed hollow point (JHP) have not resulted in any spectacular expansion over other hollow point designs, and even though the muzzle velocity of the .45 ACP cartridge is relatively low, I seriously doubt that the assailant can see if the bullet traveling in his direction looks mean. Base your ammo selection on performance, not appearance.)

Older Rounds

Older .45 ACP JHP loads did not offer great expansion, but they did offer a blunt impact point. In theory, the blunt point should deliver more shock than a round-nose bullet and cut a more defined wound channel.

An older hollow point design that worked as well or better than others of its era was the Remington 185 grain. This round was not excessively hot (enough to damage your pistol) but was surely a full-powered round. It featured a good shape conducive to reliable feeding and had a jacket that was heavy enough to withstand feed ramp abuse without deforming and causing feeding problems.

The original Remington hollow point appeared to have a hexagonal hole in the nose. While this probably had no benefit in expansion, the round did have a distinctive look and was easy to recognize when you were shopping for ammunition. An intelligent cannelure was given to the case rather than the bullet and prevented the bullet from pushing back into the case when the round went through the feeding cycle. (Such cannelured cases are still preferred in autopistols which head-space on the case mouth. Cases overcrimped at the mouth can result in improper head-spacing, and cases that don't hold the bullet sufficiently tight can allow the bullets to push back into the case during the feeding cycle.)

Do not confuse the Remington 185-grain JHP with the Remington 185-grain target wadcutter, the latter of which was specifically designed for paper punching. The target load is too light for general defensive use and the bullet is poorly designed and unreliable. In my opinion, the same is true of Federal's Gold Medal target 185-grain wadcutters.

The Remington 185-grain hollow point evolved into a load featuring Plus P velocities and pressures.

Bullet Profile

At last, obtaining a reliable feeding profile on bullet shape has become a major priority, with hollow point advancements being made by Federal, Remington, and Winchester. (A reliable bullet profile that ensures smooth feeding has always been a critical factor.) The latest generation of Federal's HYDRA-SHOK JHP, Winchester's SXT JHP, and Remington's Golden Saber JHP all feature a design suited to reliable feeding. All three are available in what could be considered logical .45 ACP loads in terms of recoil. The penetration and expansion of these newly designed bullets is quite consistent, but each shooter is going to have to perform his own evaluation. When these hollow points were compared to a hardball load in less-than-scientific water-jug test, they expanded well and stopped in the third water jug. The hardball load did not expand and ended its penetration in the seventh jug. While these loads are sufficiently accurate for moderate range, the penetration issue will have to be weighed by the shooter.

All of these loads could be improved with cannelured cartridge cases and a sealed primer, which would increase durability.

.45 ACP cartridges. L to R: HG #68 200-grain semiwadcutter, 230-grain round-nose lead, 230-grain FMJ, and 230-grain HYDRA-SHOK.

The 230-grain .45 ACP flat point has been considered an option by some. The round's diameter provides a large caliber profile and the flat, blunt point can transmit additional impact shock to the target. These bullets are available in FMJ as well as hard-cast lead. However, I have evaluated the Hornady factory 230-grain FMJ flat point and found that the noncannelured case allows bullet setback during multiple chamberings. This problem, until cured, eliminates it from consideration.

The Hensly and Gibbs (HG) #68 semiwadcutter design is a very popular bullet and widely used in .45 ACP practical competition. It is a lead 200-grain bullet with a long nose and a sharp shoulder near the mouth of the case. Some experienced shooters carry this bullet in once-fired cases with a full-power powder charge and Federal primers. Extremely experienced reloaders who are genuinely capable of loading reliable defensive ammunition can assure that every primer has an anvil and every cartridge case has a primer flash hole. The precision of a professional hand-loader goes a long way toward being confident in this cartridge's reliability. Individual gauging of each and every loaded cartridge will ensure that its outside dimensions are correct and it will chamber when needed.

The HG #68 feeds very reliably in properly throated autopistols and is an extremely accurate bullet. The bullet's sharp shoulder and clean hole punching ability would probably work very well in a defensive situation, as do semiwadcutter hunting bullets. (The semiwadcutter relies on a sharp, full-diameter shoulder cutting a .45 caliber hole rather than depending on expansion. Hunters who have used this bullet design are aware of its ability to cut a sharp hole and leave a substantial blood trail, rather than simply push through a torso, such as a round-nose or nonexpanding hollow point might.)

There were two factory loads I am aware of that featured a FMJ or copperized HG #68-style bullet. While both were full-power loads, one featured an aluminum cartridge case and the other had problems with bullet push-back during repeated feeding cycles with the same cartridges. Although aluminum case cartridges are not recommended because of the problem with the aluminum occasionally sticking in the chamber after the round is fired, initial testing of the brass-cased FMJ was both reliable and accurate. This full-power load seemed suitable as a defensive carry cartridge, having the benefits associated with the semiwadcutter and none of the stigma that is commonly attached to hollow points. Additional detailed testing of later lots revealed inconsistent bullet push-back problems so it can not be recommended until the problem is cured. If the 200-grain HG #68 semiwadcutter FMJ had a velocity of approximately 1,000 fps with a cannelured brass case and a sealed primer, it would make an excellent .45 ACP defensive load. As of this writing, a cartridge with all of these features is not known to be available.

While truly experienced hand loaders can produce ammunition superior in accuracy to factory-loaded ammunition for a particular handgun, all too often some hand loaders overrate their ability, which leads to substandard ammunition in terms of function and accuracy. One should be extremely critical of his own efforts in this area.

Naturally, there are liability concerns with reloads. Selecting and carrying a factory loaded cartridge effectively limits the claim that the shooter was trying to make his personal ammunition more deadly than what he could purchase in a store. While nothing may be further from the truth, people experienced in modern court proceedings can easily envision such an accusation. All courtroom arguments, of course, have a counterargument, which in this case is increased reliability and accuracy, but it is probably best to simply select a factory cartridge.

Gauge all your cartridges before use.

Safety Recalls

Safety recall notices are occasionally issued by ammunition manufacturers, and some are quite serious. Networking with other firearm professionals allows you to keep your finger on the pulse of developing areas of concern, meaning you might receive notice of a problem from an associate before the manufacturer notifies you. For example, in 1996 a notice from a firearm professional was issued to range masters that case heads were being blown off .40 S&W cases when fired in Glock, Smith & Wesson, and Beretta pistols. The author of the notice was requesting reports of other such incidents in order to investigate and cure the problem and notifying others about possible trouble.

Testing Ammo

Once you have selected your ammo, purchase a sufficient quantity of it (all from the same lot) and weigh a sufficient sampling to obtain an average weight. The cartridges should each then be gauged to ensure they have the proper outside dimensions for your gun's chamber. Test fire the sampling for function, night flash, and point-of-aim point-of-impact. Penetration tests in material expected to be encountered are also a very wise idea.

Once this information is established, a quantity of carry ammunition should be taken from the same lot and individually weighed with an accurate digital scale for comparison to the ammunition sampling just fired and found to be okay. Any cartridge weighing outside the accepted variance zone should be discarded because it could mean a heavy, light, or nonexistent powder charge, among other things. Each cartridge should then be gauged for proper overall dimensions.

Checking ammunition for a primer anvil and flash hole is impossible unless all the cartridges are disassembled, which is not recommended. You won't be covering all of the bases, but you will be minimizing the chances of a potential problem.

Ammo Storage

Your ammunition should be stored in a cool, dry place to preserve its longevity. Watertight and airtight containers are best. Quantities of ammo considered minimal by the active competition shooter could be viewed as a dangerous stockpile by the nonshooting public, so be sure to check local regulations. Also, make sure your storage location has adequate fire and theft protection.

Ammo Replacement

Your ammo in your pistol should be replaced at least bimonthly to ensure that the pistol's lubrication does not have an opportunity to adversely affect cartridge performance. An area of special concern in regard to lubricant contamination is the slide's breech face and the barrel's chamber. These areas should remain clean and dry.

Reloads

Shooters who reload their own ammunition should be especially aware of proper, safe reloading procedures. If you are not extremely experienced and proficient in this area, leave the manufacture of even your practice ammunition to the professionals. One shooting buddy offering to provide another with low-cost or no-cost ammunition as a favor should generally not be considered an ammunition manufacturing professional. Many handguns have been ruined by ammunition made by an inexperienced reloader. Trusting your own proper loads or that of a major factory is your wisest course of action.

Shooters entering the reloading field should be acquainted with Dillon Precision. This company has gained a reputation in the shooting community as a supplier of the finest in reloading equipment backed up by superior customer service. I recommend Dillon Precision over any other company when it comes to progressive reloading equipment. Dillon Precision offers reloading machines from inexpensive, moderate output machine to high capacity models for the quantity loader.

Ammunition, especially when fired from a compensated pistol, should be thoroughly tested in low-light conditions for muzzle flash.

Dillon also offers quality cartridge case tumblers, which are a necessity. Clean cases are mandatory for long-term pistol reliability. With the advent of digital reloading scales and affordable chronographing equipment, along with quality instruction and technical advice, the individual shooter can be more knowledgeable than ever before.

DEFENSIVE AMMUNITION SELECTION SUMMARY

Shooters using 230-grain hardball as an all-around defensive load for consistent reliability, power, penetration, and accuracy would be served well with Federal Match hardball for carry. Federal American Eagle hardball is a quality, yet less expensive, training and practice round. Remington 230-grain FMJ hardball is not recommended because of its demonstrated tendency to push back into the case during a repeated feed cycle.

Shooters who are concerned about overpenetration of FMJ ammo and who want direct maximum energy transfer to an unobscured/unarmored target, should consider the latest generation of hollow points by Federal, Remington, and Winchester. Federal HYDRA-SHOK, Remington Golden Saber, and Winchester SXTs all provide limited penetration and good expansion, generally speaking.

Additional developments might eventually be made with 200-grain FMJ HG #68 semiwadcutters in a cannelured case, as well as 230-grain flat points. These would be two rounds for consideration, provided they are properly developed.

Whichever round is selected, it should be thoroughly tested and evaluated prior to carry.

Reliability, penetration, night flash, recoil, expansion, and other factors specific to your environment should all be considered.

Defensive handgunners, police, and tactical officers who wear a bullet-resistant vest on a regular basis should not carry a cartridge that can penetrate that vest. In a gun snatch situation, your vest might have to stop your own rounds.

Shot placement will remain a critical factor in ending any encounter, and a "failure to stop" situation has occurred with nearly all cartridges, including those reputed to be "manstoppers." The hard lesson learned by observing all manner of shooting incidents is that there is no magic bullet and that handgun cartridges can fail to stop with surprising regularity, especially when controlled substances are involved. Proficiency and training are a must with any cartridge.

.45 ACP Factory Loads	Approximate Factory Velocity*
Winchester 230 gr. FMJ RN	835 fps
Remington 230 gr. FMJ RN	835 fps
CCI Blazer 230 gr. FMJ RN	845 fps
Hornady 230 gr. FMJ FN	850 fps
Winchester 230 gr. JHP	850 fps
Federal 230 gr. JHP	850 fps
Black Hills 230 gr. FMJ RN	850 fps
Hornady 200 gr. FMJ SWC	800 fps
Hornady 200 gr. JHP XTP	900 fps
Black Hills 200 gr. JHP	900 fps
CCI Blazer 200 gr. JHP	975 fps
Speer Lawman 200 gr. JHP	975 fps
Corbon 200 gr. JHP Plus P	1,050 fps
Hornady 185 gr. JHP STP	950 fps
Black Hills 185 gr. JHP	975 fps
Winchester 185 gr. STHP	1,000 fps
Remington 185 gr. JHP	1,000 fps
Remington 185 gr. JHP Plus P	1,140 fps
Corbon 185 gr. JHP Plus P	1,150 fps

*Velocities obtained from five-inch barrels.

Chapter 6

BASIC HANDGUN SHOOTING

No greater wrong can ever be done than to put a good man at the mercy of a bad, while telling him not to defend himself or his fellows. In no way can the success of evil be made more sure.

—Theodore Roosevelt

Once a quality pistol is obtained, loaded with proper ammunition, and sighted in, obtaining hits on your target is quite simple if you stick with the basics of good handgun shooting: proper stance, grip, sight alignment, trigger control, and follow-through.

Watching an experienced practical shooter fire might lead you to believe that he is merely pointing and shooting very quickly, which normally isn't the case. What you are seeing is a highly developed basic shooter who is simply applying the basics very quickly. To prove this, try some fast-pointed shots at a torso-sized target at relatively close range. When you find yourself missing or obtaining poor hits on the target, come back and study this chapter in detail.

I am a firm believer in thoroughly learning the basics and then developing the speed to use them quickly, and I know many bull's-eye shooters who have made the transition to practical competition shooting. Once their speed develops, their basic shooting discipline is quite evident in the fact that they are still shooting very accurately, but with substantial speed.

SIGHTING IN

Before you get started shooting your pistol please review the applicable safety rules as well as the operational rules of the 1911.

The pistol needs to be sighted in straight-away. You may want to function fire your pistol before you get super serious about sighting in, but sighting in comes immediately afterward. Going straight into match shooting or street carry of a defensive pistol without sighting it in sounds ludicrous, but many people do it. A nonzeroed pistol can cost you match points on the range, and, more importantly, a life on the street.

Loading

Load only from a loaded magazine. Do not drop single rounds directly into the chamber and close the slide because the extractor on the 1911 is not a pivoting style extractor; requiring it to snap over rounds placed directly into the chamber can affect the adjustment of and even fracture the extractor hook. So, load the pistol by inserting a magazine, racking the slide, engaging the manual thumb safety, and topping off the magazine with another round.

Do not allow the slide to slam shut empty. There is no logical excuse for doing so, and it just batters your pistol unnecessarily. With a loaded magazine locked in place, it is fine to allow the slide to go forward under its own spring pressure and chamber the round, but there is no reason for slamming it empty. On a pistol with the last-shot lock-open feature eliminated, or when the pistol is unintentionally shot dry, the convex magazine follower will slow the slide to approximately the same speed as when chambering a round, which minimizes any battering of the barrel lugs.

If you want the slide to go home empty, hold on to the slide, disengage the slide stop, and carefully let the slide go forward without allowing it to slam.

Operators

Don't abuse your equipment, and make sure that anyone using your equipment is very well versed in safe gun handling and the operation of the 1911 before you allow them to handle the pistol.

The pistol's primary operator should be the person who fine tunes the sight-in. Pre-modification conferences with your pistolsmith should be enough for him to sight in the pistol very close to your particular ammo and sight hold. You should still check the pistol on paper just to confirm the zero.

Zero Distances

The distance you zero your pistol at should be determined by the ranges you are most likely to encounter in the field. Some tactical officers like their pistol zeroed at five yards so that they need no compensation for a close-range head shot. Other shooters zero their 1911s at 100 yards. While torso size hits can be regularly obtained by a proficient shooter with a quality autopistol out to 200 yards, it is probably wiser to keep your pistol zeroed closer to normal distances, such as 15 to 25 yards, although competition shooters go out to 50 yards. But no matter what distance you choose to zero your pistol at, you should know where it impacts at other ranges and know the necessary sight holds to compensate for trajectory. For example, if you zero your pistol for 15 yards to impact precisely where you aim, you should also take the time to set out targets from point blank to at least 50 yards and check the impacts, just as an experienced precision marksman does with his rifle from zero to 1,000 yards. Unfortunately, many shooters don't think that trajectory patterning is important for pistols. As your shooting experience increases, you will probably recognize the benefits of trajectory patterning. Reality dictates that in combat situations you are not going to have time to count clicks on your adjustable sight; you will have to instantly know what sight picture will give you a hit at all feasible ranges. Gaining this information and developing skill comes from dedicated range time. Don't expect all armed encounters to occur at less than seven yards and present you with a full-size target, because most people tend to make very small targets of themselves behind cover when the shooting starts. (This should also be true of the defensive shooter who is well practiced in taking cover.) Successfully completing a hostage rescue shot or shooting an assailant who is mostly behind hard cover requires precision shooting skills.

Sight Picture

The sight picture hold is an important issue to discuss with your pistolsmith. If your smith normally sights in with a point-of-impact hold and you sight in with a six o'clock hold, there will be a substantial difference in point-of-impact. Whereas competition shooters may elect to zero their pistols with a six o'clock hold on a 12-inch bull's-eye target, the defensive shooter must be more realistic. As stated

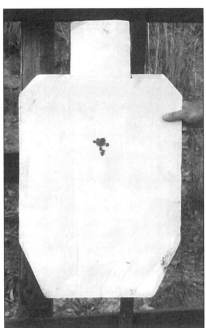

A solid rest helps to show a new shooter that the pistol is indeed accurate.

earlier, fixed sights are quite adjustable for point-of-impact, but the smith needs to know load and hold information to properly adjust them to your needs.

I prefer a point-of-aim point-of-impact hold with a 15- to 25-yard zero. This means that to align the sights with the target you put the target right on top of the front sight, i.e., use a six o'clock hold on the exact spot (no larger than the bullet's diameter) you want to hit. This type of zero is preferred over the six o'clock hold on a 12-inch bull's-eye because the latter forces you to concentrate on an aiming point that is six inches below the area you actually want to hit. This gets very confusing and becomes time consuming when you are shooting fast and estimating ranges and sight holds. (Never set up your equipment in a way that detracts from your concentration.)

A good technique is to place a half-inch dot on a target at your zero distance and then set the dot directly on top of the front sight during the alignment process. This way the precise aiming point can be acquired for a tight shot group, but it is still basically a point-of-aim point-of-impact zero when the shooting becomes fast at less defined targets.

Important: Don't start adjusting your sight until you are consistently firing tight, rested, slow-fire groups. Too many shooters decide to start changing their sight adjustment when they are still shooting a substantially large group pattern. A shooter can't possibly logically decide which way to move the sight when rounds are impacting all over the target.

If you are not shooting good groups and the pistol/ammunition combination is not at fault (which it rarely is with beginning shooters), go back to the basics. Make sure you are shooting from a solid, well-supported position, and don't try to shoot sight-in groups from the offhand position (there is simply too much human error involved in unsupported positions).

Most new pistol shooters tend to shoot low when learning to shoot, with the right-handed shooter firing low and left and the left-handed shooter firing low and right. New shooters tend to believe the pistol is sighted in low and want to adjust the elevation accordingly. With a new shooter, in most instances it is a case of dipping the muzzle the instant they break the shot. Combining muzzle dip with a right- or left-hand trigger pull will place the shot pattern low and left or low and

The Weaver stance (left) and isosceles stance (right) can both be adapted for use in a variety of situations.

right. And the new shooter who has no concept of sight alignment and trigger control will shoot all over, on and off the target.

One of the first steps in correcting a shooting problem is for the shooter to acknowledge that there is a human skill problem factored into the situation. Blaming an "inaccurate" or "unzeroed" pistol is common with new shooters. In the case of the new shooter hitting low because of muzzle dip, an experienced shooter may have to fire the pistol to demonstrate its grouping capability before the new shooter will acknowledge the problem. Videotaping the new shooter and playing the shooting sequence back in slow motion will show the shooter the pistol's movement the instant before firing.

A ball and dummy exercise is another method of demonstrating this problem. Here, the instructor loads the magazine with live and dummy cartridges without allowing the shooter to see the order. When the shooter pulls the trigger on a dummy cartridge and there is no recoil to mask the muzzle dip, the problem becomes obvious.

Once the pistol is properly sighted in from a rested position and the shooter knows the pistol is precisely sighted in, he should acknowledge any misses as resulting from human error.

As soon as the shot is released, experienced shooters have a very good idea where the bullet is going to hit. This is known as calling the shot. Shooting experience tells you if you have correctly completed the basics on each and every shot. Finally, never adjust the sights to compensate for a shooting problem. If you are not doing well, don't make excuses. Correct problems by practicing the basics and getting additional assistance if necessary.

STANCE

Learning to use an effective shooting stance is important when it comes to the basics of all types of shooting. While sight alignment and trigger control are the most critical factors in delivering accurate shots, stance is an important consideration because it puts the shooter in a better position to handle the overall situation.

Transitioning from the low ready to target acquisition in the Weaver stance.

The recoil your pistol generates often influences stance, especially during rapid fire. A new shooter should try various stances and positions and find what works well for his body style and restrictions.

Isosceles

The isosceles stance works well for some shooters, but for the most part it works best with low-recoil pistols that are fired slowly, although there are exceptions. Rapid fire of a heavier recoiling pistol should be considered when choosing your stance. Many top level competitors use the isosceles stance, but the firearms they use are quite often compensated to reduce recoil and muzzle flip.

The isosceles stance got its name because the shooter forms an isosceles triangle with his arms and body. I find it doesn't work particularly well during close rapid fire with a full-power pistol. It is also a questionable stance for shooters who must fire high-speed, close-range shots at one assailant while in physical contact with another assailant. This should be a major consideration for the combat shooter who could be operating at close quarters. Experiment with it and use it if it meets all your requirements. I use a variation of the isosceles in a modified thumbs-up grip for more precise, longer range offhand shooting where hands-on activity won't be a factor.

Weaver

The Weaver stance, or one of its many modern variations, is popular among today's full-power, noncompensated combat pistol shooters. One of its variations uses a two-handed hold with the strong arm almost straight and the support arm's elbow bent and held close to the body. The strong-side foot is usually half a step back and the weak-side foot is forward. The body is angled to the target area like a boxer's stance. This stance allows the shooter's upper body to act as a turret and cover a large area. In their respective positions, the arms do well to control even heavy recoil handguns, and proper positioning of the shooter's feet allows for quick movement for addressing shooting problems or applying physical countermeasures.

A modified Weaver stance is effective for most quick and close shooting. At contact distances, a fending one-hand position or a speed rock-and-draw is used; just outside of physical contact distance (one to three yards), a close-in, two-handed position is used with both arms bent. As distance increases, so does the need for a solid stance and greater extension of both arms. Bringing the sights on target is recommended at any distance past gun grabbing range. A defensive shooter must, of course, realize the effect of action versus reaction in terms of time and the distance an assailant can cover during one's reaction time.

I find a modified, sights-on-target Weaver stance works very well from just past contact range to approximately 20 yards. Beyond 20 yards, when shooting at relatively precise targets, more of a locked arm stance may prove better. For beyond 20 yards, I prefer the strong arm to be locked out along with the weak arm that supports it. This dual locked arm position is very similar to the isosceles stance. The strong-hand thumb remains consistent in its high thumb hold. The weak-hand thumb moves forward and down to a contact point on the frame just in front of the slide stop, which allows for inward tension by both hands to stabilize the pistol and achieve precise sight alignment. This opposing inward pressure also allows the shooter to control even a carry-weight trigger while keeping the sights fully aligned.

Distance to the target and the precision needed to make the shot dictate how much of a supportive position and controlled trigger press is necessary. Close and fast shooting at moderate size targets certainly does not require as rigid a support platform as distant and precise targets do. With experience, the shooter will learn how much support and trigger control is necessary to achieve hits on targets of various sizes and at various ranges.

Precision handgun shooting can be very effectively used at extreme close range by proficient shooters making a quick and close, no-reflex zone shot. This could serve the defensive shooter much better than simply delivering torso hits on an assailant. If the distance is close and the assailant is serious about achieving his goal, an instant shutdown of the assailant's actions could be critical to the survival of the defender.

The modified Weaver stance, which works very well at moderate ranges, also lends itself to a two-handed low ready position, which is sometimes referred to as the guard position. From the low ready position a shooter can observe the target area, move easily while remaining balanced, and still deliver quick shots, but the position can be exaggerated to the point that time is wasted and excessive distance is covered to bring the sights back onto target.

The shooter will have to decide how low of a ready position is called for. The shooter who brings a weapon from the ultra-low ready into a sighted firing position will no doubt telegraph impending action, and the action/reaction factor must be considered. Regardless of the position, the shooter must not cover a potential target from view with his own arm and weapon. This is especially important when descending stairwells.

One- and Weak-Handed Shooting

Although two-handed shooting is always preferred, one- and weak-handed shooting should be practiced because of the possibility of injury and the need to operate support equipment. Recoil and muzzle flip feel much different when shooting one-handed and especially when the weak hand is used. Learn techniques that work for you and make any compensation necessary for increased accuracy.

New shooters shouldn't assume that they have to shoot exactly like other top competitors or instructors. While certain stances and techniques enjoy clear popularity, shooting is an ever-developing arena where experimentation often leads to more effective techniques. Always seek to expand your knowledge and develop your shooting skills to the highest level possible.

The Expert

Now is a good time to cover the term *expert*. Expert can indicate a level or score one has achieved on a shooting course and can also be applied to people who have shown that they are very knowledgeable in a particular field. The term may be accepted as a firearms rating, but I don't believe true expert or master status is attainable in a field that is always developing. Therefore, beware of shooting instructors who insist they have attained an all-knowing level. Additionally, people with big egos often fall short in both performance and experience. This type of instructor will oftentimes be intimidated by those who do well and hence try to stifle their success. The best shooters are those who are always learning and developing.

Quality shooting instructors aren't rigid in every aspect of their training and encourage safe freestyle experimentation. I believe shooting students should learn all they can from as many people as they can, separate the good techniques from the ineffective, and develop their own shooting style. Looking like a firing-line clone is not a requirement; hitting the target is. In any case, your shooting skills will probably progress much faster under the guidance of a competent instructor, and serious thought should be put into your selection of one because incompetent instructors are becoming more and more common.

The shooter must determine exactly what type of firearms training he is interested in. The primary thrust of this book is toward the defensive handgunner, so the recommended schools and instructors in the back of this book provide handgun instruction primarily in this area.

Switching from your strong hand to your weak hand immediately after the draw is easily accomplished. Be sure not to cover your weak hand with the muzzle during the draw or transfer. The situation will dictate whether the manual thumb safety should be disengaged during the transfer.

A good shooting instructor doesn't necessarily have to be a world-class shooting competitor, especially because many shooting competitions are based on what many consider to be impractical courses of fire and firearms that are unrealistic for street use and carry. In short, excellent competition shooters/instructors may have little knowledge of street tactics, and instructor credibility is an important consideration because of the high probability of litigation following a gunfight. It is unwise to attend handgun training programs presented by an individual or individuals of questionable character and later expect to present them in a court of law as credible witnesses.

GRIP

When I speak of the shooter's grip, I am not talking about the stocks on the pistol but rather the shooter's grip on them.

It is important to have a pistol that fits or has been modified to fit the shooter's hands by using the proper stocks, checkering, mainspring housing, and beavertail. A good grip is very firm but isn't a death grip, which causes the shooter to tremble. Some shooters like the two-handed hold with one finger wrapped around the front of the trigger guard, and others like the two-handed hold with the index finger of the support hand under the trigger guard. Some shooters prefer a high thumb hold with both thumbs on top of the safety, and others prefer to lock both thumbs below the manual thumb safety.

Two-Handed

A two-handed hold with the weak-hand index finger held under the trigger guard helps the shooter avoid dipping the muzzle when breaking the shot. For shooters (especially new shooters) with a muzzle dipping problem, I highly recommend trying this grip. Experienced shooters increasing their speed will also find this grip to be beneficial during rapid fire, because it provides sight picture stability all the way through the release of the shot. I also prefer the weak-hand index finger under the trigger guard because it establishes a firm wedged position of the fingers. However, horizontal serrations on the front of the trigger guard are still desirable, because when the support hand doesn't wind up in a perfect position and the weak-hand index finger lands on the front of the trigger guard during a fast draw, the shot can be quickly taken while in a secure position without wasting time repositioning the support hand; the serrations help keep the support-hand index finger in place to dampen muzzle flip.

Varying Your Grip

Shooting from all positions with various grips should be experienced during serious range training so that some sense of familiarity is attained; a genuine potentially deadly situation should not be the first time you experience a certain shooting position or grip. (Proper preparation will always be the primary factor in consistent success.) In a shootout, after the initial shots are made and there is a brief break in the action, the preferred hand grip should be reestablished on the weapon.

The High Grip

The shooter should attempt to maintain the pistol deeply seated in his two-handed hold, establishing a very high and firm grip to reduce muzzle flip and maintain his sight picture for follow-up shots and allowing him to have the pistol in a ready position with the safety on. The shooter should draw the weapon with the thumb on top of the thumb safety so that when the pistol is brought into a firing position, the thumb safety can be released and the pistol fired without unnecessary delay. This also allows the shooter to have the safety engaged until the instant of firing the pistol, which is very important should the shooter have to hold an attacker at gunpoint or grapple with someone. The safety should always be in its on position unless the pistol is being fired. Once this technique is ingrained in the shooter, he will find it possible to maintain the pistol in a

Both thumbs below the manual thumb safety aren't recommended either, because of additional time being needed to get them there and the fact that the safety could be bumped on during recoil.

condition with the manual safety engaged during all searches, movement, and suspect contacts until firing is required.

The shooter will fire with his strong-hand thumb on top of the manual thumb safety to eliminate any delay when the shooter finds it necessary to reposition his thumbs below the thumb safety before firing. Firing with the thumb on top of the thumb safety also eliminates the possibility of accidentally bumping the thumb safety into its engaged position during rapid fire. (Do not follow the foolish advice of applying pressure to the trigger and then disengaging the thumb safety, causing the pistol to fire.) Proper thumb safety operation will come with ease when using the 1911, which is designed to allow operation of the manual thumb safety while in a firing grip. The argument that a shooter will forget to release a manual thumb safety in a high-speed defensive encounter and therefore be better served by a point-and-pull pistol is simply a training issue. A shooter who isn't willing to train with his particular choice of handgun shouldn't carry any handgun. Shooters properly trained to operate the manual thumb safety of the 1911 will find it an extremely natural design, which is greatly preferred over the slide-mounted decocking/safety levers of some poorly designed autopistols. (These autopistols don't position the thumb lever well for quick combat use, hence the safety is seldom used during dangerous encounters for fear of delayed response time.)

The benefits of the high thumb grip are so great that it deserves serious consideration for anyone looking for the best grip for handling the 1911 in combat situations. It has repeatedly proven itself to be safe, fast, and effective.

SIGHT ALIGNMENT

Once the pistol is sighted in and a proper grip is obtained, the next step is aligning the sights. Target size and distance determine how precise the sights must be aligned, i.e., delivering quick shots into a torso-size target at five yards requires much less sight picture precision than a small target at extended range. On the close target you could get a reliable quick hit by using only a "flash" sight picture. More distant targets require a more precise aim and greater trigger control, and the shooter must be knowledgeable enough to compensate for bullet trajectory.

Sight Picture

Getting the correct sight picture for different ranges goes back to your sight-in homework: you should already have established and memorized the different holds for different range targets. The sights should be aligned with the front sight level with the top of the rear blade and centered in the notch. The point of focus should be the front sight; the target should fade to a fuzzy outline. (Keeping a focus on the front sight allows you to see where your rounds are impacting.)

This attention to the front sight is often one of the most difficult concepts a new shooter has to deal with, especially a defensive shooter because an aggressive threat is going to be a substantial attention grabber. Asking a defensive shooter to allow this item of immense interest to be replaced by concentration on the front sight can be a

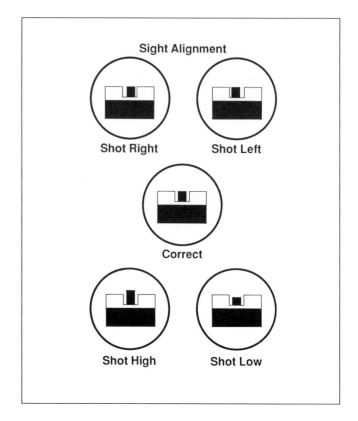

Sight alignment.

difficult area in which to gain shooter compliance. Once a shooter realizes that he cannot miss fast enough to stop the aggressor, he will want to learn how to avoid missing the target.

Reactive targets are one of the best training aides to deliver the very important lesson of sight focus. Steel reactive targets of small to moderate size that fall when impacted draw the new shooter's interest. The new shooter may be so interested in seeing the target react that he does not properly align the sights and focus on the front sight. Instead, he will often look over the sights to watch the target's reaction. The shooter will eventually learn that targets reliably go down when the proper sight alignment, sight focus, and trigger control are applied, and he will certainly learn that attempting to focus on small- to moderate-size targets and point shooting will be ineffective in most situations.

Note: Whereas point shooting may be effective in specific (lucky) instances or by highly trained point shooters, for shooting past point blank distances proper use of the sights is much more effective.

Focusing on your front sight with one eye closed, both eyes open, or a combination thereof will be determined by your eyesight. Many shooters tend to focus on the front sight with their dominant eye and just slightly squint their weak eye, while still obtaining visual input from the weak eye. As soon as your front sight recovers from recoil and gets back on target, you will be able to confirm that sight alignment is proper for the target size and range, thus making accurate follow-up shots possible.

Compensator-equipped pistols or otherwise properly modified 1911s that facilitate a high firing grip allow shooters to control muzzle flip to the point that the sight moves off target very little, if any, during recoil. When confronted by a determined adversary, getting fast multiple hits could be a critical survival skill.

Consistently hitting multiple targets requires all the basics of pistol marksmanship and a properly modified pistol.

Accurate rapid fire can be learned through dedicated practice.

The Double Tap

Close-range targets where a flash sight picture is all that is necessary can often be well addressed with the double-tap ("hammer") technique which, when combined with a flash sight picture, allows the shooter to deliver two extremely fast, accurate shots using the single flash sight picture. However, this technique should be limited to targets of moderate size at relatively close range.

The Controlled Pair

Targets beyond the effective range of the double tap can often be addressed with a controlled-pair technique. This involves the shooter obtaining sufficient sight alignment to achieve a hit on a more distant mid-sized target or a smaller close-range target and deliver a single shot followed by a quick realignment of the sights (including alignment confirmation) before following with the second shot.

The Adamant Adversary

Sustaining rapid fire on a target until reaction is obtained may be required in some situations. In modern America, encountering body armor on an adversary shouldn't be a surprise. Sustaining fire into one area of the adversary that is having no immediate effect can continue until the defender's pistol is empty, resulting in injury to the defender by an aggressive attacker. A better technique for engaging an attacker who is not being affected by impacting rounds because of body armor or drug/alcohol use can be two shots to center mass followed by a shot or shots to the head. This does create a slight break in firing, but this break is almost imperceivable when done by a proficient shooter. If the adversary is close and the shooter proficient, he may opt to go with direct head shots and bypass the body shots altogether, which is popular with tactical officers; minimize rounds fired, maximize effect.

Continuous Sight Alignment

The shooter must concentrate on sight alignment and keep a clear front sight for the entire string of fire. The only hesitation should come with the follow-up shot, when the sights come off the target because of recoil. During fast firing it is common to actually see the sights move fore and aft and the empty cases being ejected. Shooters won't be able to achieve this fast firing sight concentration if they have a problem with flinching, wincing, or eye closing during firing.

Rapid Refocusing

Sight alignment during a confrontation often requires the shooter's eyes to labor between the sights and the target and back many times. The defensive shooter must be able to watch his adversary and still come back to the sights for proper focus if necessary. Putting the target and the aiming point on the same focal plane, such as with a scope or an electronic dot sight, eliminates the need for repeated shifts in focus. However, optical sights on handguns are woefully inadequate when it comes to reliability, concealability, and durability for defensive use, making iron sights the sights of choice.

As long as the defensive shooter is aware of the rapid changes in focus he will be required to use, eye exercises a possibility. Focusing on an object at handgun-encounter distance and then rapidly refocusing on an object at arm's length is a good exercise if done on a regular basis.

Rapid refocusing skills are crucial when using an iron-sighted pistol and must be practiced to become second nature. Avoid practicing and training exclusively with an optic-sighted comp pistol if you are going to be using iron sights in the field. Shoot what you carry. (New classifications in practical shooting pistol matches dedicated to the defensive handgunner are now available for those with a competitive interest who use iron sights.) I highly recommend the one-pistol one-sight system.

Increased Ranges

Accurate long-distance shooting can certainly be achieved with a handgun by a knowledgeable shooter. Naturally, raising the front sight post past the position at which it is level with the top of the rear sight blade will increase the distance at which the target can be hit, but sometimes, such as for long-distance handgun hunting, a shooter might want additional horizontal bars on the face of the front sight. Such bars give the shooter additional reference points to determine how far he is raising the front sight. Observing his impact to be either high or low will allow him to go back and make the necessary compensation from a known reference point on the front sight face. Substantial distance shooting with a handgun will, of course, require addressing of wind deflection in certain situations. These techniques are typically not a substantial concern for the defensive handgunner who usually operates at closer distances. However, they can be quite interesting and challenging to the shooter who wants to test his skill.

TRIGGER CONTROL

Once the pistol is sighted in, a proper grip is obtained, and the sights are aligned, the manner in which the trigger is pulled or pressed can make or break the shot. It doesn't matter how well the sights are lined up or how perfectly the pistol is sighted in if you yank the sights off target when you pull the trigger.

Trigger pull (press, squeeze, whatever you want to call it) requires practice to perfect. This and sight alignment are areas where shooters spend a lifetime developing their skills. The shooting level one achieves is substantially related to these two areas, and trigger control is similar to sight alignment in that the more precise the shot, the more careful the trigger pull must be. On a small target, even a small amount of sight alignment disturbance during the trigger pull will cause a miss. Conversely, on a larger target at close range, you can get away with more trigger pull sloppiness and still hit the target. With new shooters and experienced shooters, the majority of missed shots are caused by poor sight alignment and improper trigger control. The solution is to be extremely dedicated to practicing the basics of good shooting. Slow, steady practice of the basics will allow you to develop your skills, and your speed will increase with experience. Practicing a slow, steady trigger press with proper sight alignment and hold will result in a hit. The time it takes to complete these steps can be extremely short when performed by the proficient shooter.

Finger Position

Finger position on the trigger is a matter of personal preference based on performance. Many bull's-eye shooters prefer the tip of the finger to be the only part of the finger operating the trigger, but many combat shooters prefer using the first joint of the index finger. The latter gives, in most circumstances, a greater and more even pulling pressure on the trigger and works very well when pulling a carry-weight trigger, without disturbing sight alignment.

Follow-Through

Follow-through is an important component in delivering accurate shots. If the shooter allows his stance and grip to collapse at the instant the cartridge is ignited the shot will be adversely affected because of pistol disturbance during the bullet's movement down the barrel. Follow-through solves this problem by requiring the shooter to maintain a good sight picture and sight alignment throughout the firing cycle.

Dry Firing

The basics of stance, grip, sight alignment, trigger control, and follow-through can be effectively practiced without live ammunition and is known as dry firing. Use a snap cap to prevent firing pin damage when dry firing and feed the snap cap into the chamber via the magazine, which increases the longevity of your pistol). I also highly recommend that all your dry fire practice be aimed at a target with a backstop capable of stopping a bullet, even though you are not planning on shooting live ammunition. If this recommendation was followed by all, numerous "dry firings" that have sent bullets into the street would have been avoided.

Unintentional discharges involving dry firing typically occur when the shooter has established in his mind that the pistol has not been firing during his practice sessions. The shooter then loads the weapon with live ammunition and without thinking does one last segment of dry firing. This, of course, results in an unintentional discharge that is certainly the shooter's fault. This can be prevented by keeping the dry firing shooting area completely free of all ammunition, i.e., allow only practice dummy cartridges to be in the immediate area, which enables the shooter to dry fire and practice safe handgun manipulation and loading techniques. At the end of this session the shooter must mentally and physically break complete contact from the training environment and then reestablish his mind-set that there is live ammunition in the pistol and act accordingly. Dry fire practice in a setting capable of stopping live ammunition allows the shooter to practice treating all guns as if they were loaded with live ammunition.

Terminology

As your basic shooting skills develop, you will be able to achieve faster and smoother trigger releases. Your experience will tell you when you can get away with a little bit of a jerk or slap on the trigger and still hit your target, which will be determined range, target size, and time available to hit that target.

The shooting term "surprise break" (the shooter not knowing the precise moment of fire) is an understandable analogy for training the new shooter, but one I believe shouldn't be used. Should the term be presented in a post-shooting investigation or other court proceeding, the shooter might have to explain why he trained to have his defensive weapon discharge as a surprise. While knowledgeable shooters completely understand the term and the training connotation it has, it may allow the other side's attorney to muddy the issue in a courtroom. By using better terminology, the shooter will become more decisive.

"Weak hand" and "strong hand" should be reconsidered as well. For most people it is an efficient way of designating shooting hands, but such terminology can set them up for panic when they are forced to shoot with their weak hand in a live situation. Shooters should try to be as ambidextrous as possible and instructors should train their students with this in mind.

Practice As If Your Life Depends On It . . . Because It Does

Repetitive practice of the basics pays off in increased performance. When you are missing, slow down a notch and concentrate on the basics. I recommend that each practice session have a segment of basic sighted shooting skills incorporated into it. This refamiliarizes the shooter with a perishable critical skill and allows him to confirm the zero on the pistol from a solid rested position. Practice the basics often and they will become a good habit you can depend on.

The fundamentals of accurate shooting are no secret; they have been around as long as accurate firearms. A competitor is most likely able to outshoot you because he is more dedicated to the fundamentals and match preparation than you are. Street encounters have other tactical issues factored in that determine their outcome, including a host of elements right down to and including dumb luck. But, as the saying goes, "the more I practice and prepare, the luckier I seem to get."

Dedicate yourself to serious training in fundamental pistolcraft and you will become a very effective shooter.

Chapter 7

ADVANCED HANDGUN SKILLS

As your skill with a handgun progresses, you should continue developing even more of a shooting edge. The firearms arena, especially the advanced shooting field, is under constant development and refinement in the quest for better performance. There are some extremely knowledgeable and proficient shooters out there, and you should become familiar with as many shooting styles as possible. Learn and use what works for you and disregard the rest. Never be satisfied with basic performance and always try to shoot with people at or above your skill level. (Advanced shooters who find themselves saddled with a poorly skilled instructor or shooting partner often notice a deterioration of their skills by the end of the training session.)

Instructors and range masters who are unfamiliar with the high-speed, low-drag techniques of the modern professional handgunner may view him as a danger on the range because he operates with speed substantially beyond that of the average shooter. Whereas speed without skill can certainly be dangerous, too often a safe and highly skilled shooter is handicapped by range or instructor rules designed for the inexperienced plinker. It is very important for the shooter to establish a safe range location accustomed to professional handgunning techniques. The training academies located in the back of this book provide arenas for safe, high-speed defensive handgun instruction.

Once you learn the basics, you will need to develop your speed, reloading ability, smooth draw, position shooting, one-handed shooting, malfunction training, and tactics for defensive encounters.

THE DRAW

A smooth draw adds to your overall speed and does more for your ability to hit quickly with the first shot than does trying to be overly aggressive on the draw. An aggressive draw seems faster to the person making the draw, but it actually makes the shooter tense up and not move as fast. This can typically be seen in the shooter trying to overcome his own rigidity in getting the pistol aligned on target. The aggressive need for speed in a tense shooter is also commonly seen when a shooter's tense grip doesn't allow the trigger to reset enough after the first shot to trigger the next shot. (Also, although movement to the pistol must be swift and allow for a solid grip, there is no need to try to overmuscle it, which interferes with a smooth presentation.) When this happens with a 1911, you know the shooter is tense because the trigger reset distance is relatively short. Pistols with longer trigger pulls present even more of a problem. A double-action revolver, for example, can be double clutched, results in a skipped chamber. This, of course, can throw the shooting sequence off, which commonly happens to shooters who are not used to handling the pressure of high-speed firearm competition.

The draw from the standard belt carry uses the same steps as the draw from the duty holster. Remember, straight to the gun and straight to the target with no wasted motion.

The pressure or stress in a live encounter may or may not be felt even more by the defensive shooter, so tensing problems must be thoroughly evaluated in training sessions. They can be overcome with dedicated practice and the achievment of a confident skill level under pressure. Contrary to what the anti-gun mentality likes to promote—that the proficient

shooter is a gun nut and is likely to overreact in an attempt to use a firearm to end a situation—normally the opposite is true. The shooter who is confident that he can react with proficiency at high speed in a stressful encounter will be less likely to fire unnecessarily. Conversely, the shooter who is aware of his lack of training, proficiency, and ability with a firearm in or out of high-stress encounters will be more likely to begin firing unnecessarily in an effort to compensate for his poor skills.

Starting Position

A starting position common in modern pistol competition is the surrender position, which requires the shooter to start with his hands in a near equal position to other competitors, just above the shoulders. Although this technique can be incorporated into street distraction tactics and one should be familiar with it, it shouldn't be the only hand position that is practiced prior to the actual drawing of the pistol.

Another competition-driven position associated with the surrender position is cocking the head and staring at the holstered pistol in concentration prior to the draw. This maneuver may or may not work well in competition, but of course is not a sound street practice.

Economy of Motion

Economy of motion—moving straight to the holstered pistol, snatching it out of the holster, and punching it straight to the target—proves much faster than sweeping the pistol toward the target. Sweeping the pistol up to the target or rainbowing the pistol down to target level is wasted motion and should be avoided. By going straight to the holstered pistol, positively clearing the muzzle from the holster (without overclearing it), and punching the pistol straight out to the target using a proper grip and stance achieves the best results. This economy of motion allows the pistol's sights to be observed as the pistol is punched toward the target and initial alignment is made. By the time the pistol is locked out, sight alignment need only be confirmed before the shot is fired.

THE FIVE-STEP DRAW

Drawing can be broken down into five steps.

1. Grasp the pistol with the thumb on top of the safety and the trigger finger outside the trigger guard and positively clear the weapon from the holster. Keep the support hand clear of the muzzle.
2. As the pistol moves forward, bring the support hand into position from the side without it going in front of the muzzle. Attain a proper two-handed grip.
3. Punch the weapon out from the body and up to eye level with correct body/weapon alignment and initial sight alignment.
4. Positively identify the target and reconfirm the threat level and sight alignment. Move the thumb safety to the off position.
5. Complete the trigger pull without disturbing sight alignment for each shot. Remember that the hand goes straight to the pistol and the weapon goes straight to the target with no wasted motion.

Drawing from the holster and shooting single, multiple, or moving targets requires the shooter to use a smooth, consistent, well-practiced draw. It is necessary for the shooter to get a good firing grip on the pistol in the holster. This allows the shooter to complete his entire string of fire without having to change his grip during the string. Changing your grip after the draw not only reduces the speed of your first hit, but fails to help you concentrate on the follow-up shots.

To be consistent, a shooter needs much practice on drawing the pistol and aligning the sights. Practicing with proper technique will result in good hit probability, and your speed will increase with experience. Plus, consistent practice will result in muscle memory during times of stress. Don't try to be too fast too soon, and don't get frustrated if speed and accuracy don't come right away. Some shooters progress faster than others, but nearly every able person can eventually learn to shoot well.

Note: A concealed-carry, strong-side draw is completed the same as the standard five-step draw with the addition of a coat sweep. The small finger on the strong hand briskly sweeps the coat clear of the pistol while the shooter rotates his strong-side hip slightly forward and acquires the pistol with the strong hand.

Surprise can be one of your biggest allies when wearing your pistol concealed, so do not inadvertently allow your pistol to be viewed. In some locales, simply flashing a holstered pistol can be considered brandishing a weapon or menacing another person. A police officer in plainclothes who carries a concealed pistol may want to have his badge in the same area as his holstered pistol. This way, when a draw from concealment is completed the badge will be observable at the same time. Identification could be a critical factor in the outcome of a situation.

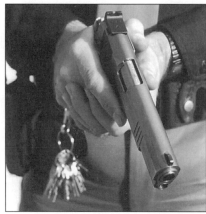

The five-step draw.

HOLSTER DESIGN

The reason for selecting the best holster becomes quite obvious when you practice your draw-and-fire routine. If the holster doesn't allow you to get a good, complete firing grip on the pistol when it is holstered to its full depth, you will have to adjust your grip after the pistol has been drawn, which results in wasted time. The holster design you choose should allow you to get a full grip on the pistol.

If your holster requires that you use two hands to reholster the pistol, get a better holster. If your holster requires you to reach across and spread the security strap open for reholstering, you may inadvertently sweep your hand or have difficulty reholstering when your support hand is busy. A shooter not cognizant of muzzle control usually spreads the holster open and brings the muzzle over the top of the support hand when reholstering. The proper procedure is to go around the support hand and come into the held-open holster from the rear.

It is critical for the operator to be familiar with his holster, especially when using selective security devices. A disastrous delay in the draw can result if one is not knowledgeable and skilled with his holster.

Thigh Holsters

Low-mounted thigh tactical holsters commonly used by SWAT teams present their own unique problems and advantages. The security devices may or may not be adequate to retain the pistol during tactical use, and even holsters that do retain the pistol securely in the holster must have the proper straps

When wearing a concealment garment, place something heavy, such as a set of keys, in the front pocket. This makes the garment easier to sweep back.

to ensure that the entire rig doesn't severely flop around on the leg while running. The best low-mounted thigh holster at this time is the Safariland rig.

A Holster Safety Note

Do not disengage the thumb safety while the pistol is still holstered. Many shooters do this in hope of picking up a little speed on the first shot. This doesn't work and is unsafe. You have already disengaged the grip safety when you grip the pistol and must not disengage the thumb safety until the pistol is pointed in a safe direction (keep your finger off of the trigger, too). This is another advantage of the high thumb hold in that it allows the shooter to have the thumb safety activated until ready to fire, with no loss in speed.

SPEED RELOAD

The speed at which a shooter can reload follows the same lines as the draw: a smooth, consistent reload using economy of motion is faster than trying to muscle the magazine into the pistol. Tension on the reload slows you down and has a good chance of causing a lockup or a fumbled reload. Whereas it is true that a beveled or enlarged magazine well helps facilitate a smooth reload, nothing can substitute for proper technique.

The most effective way I have found to reload quickly is to position the strong hand so it can easily activate the magazine release button. (The amount of hand repositioning, if any, will vary depending upon the style of magazine release button and hand size.) With the finger outside the trigger guard, confirm that a fresh magazine is available, hit the magazine release button with the strong-hand thumb, grab a fresh magazine with the weak hand, and position the weak-hand index finger on the nose of the top round in the fresh magazine. Now use the weak-hand index finger to index the fresh magazine against the inside rear of the magazine well and seat the magazine with the palm of the weak hand. If you have fired the pistol dry and the slide has locked to the rear, rotate the weak hand back up into firing position and release the slide stop with the thumb of the weak hand.

If the last-shot lock-open feature has been deactivated and the shooter has not fired the pistol dry, it is simply a matter of ejecting the spent magazine and replacing it with a fresh one. If there is a brief break in the action in lighted conditions, the chamber can be checked visually using the observation port in the barrel hood, or a press check can be used. In darkness, the press check can be completed by feel.

If the last-shot lock-open feature has been eliminated and the shooter has fired the pistol dry or is unsure if the chamber is loaded, the shooter can simply seat the magazine and rack the slide as a part of the reloading procedure. This may eject a live round from the chamber, but it will ensure the shooter that the pistol has a loaded chamber. Using an illuminator round, as previously discussed, at the bottom of the magazine can reduce reloading confusion.

An experienced 1911 shooter develops an amazing ability to sense the ammunition load left in his pistol. This comes from dedicated shooting with a specific capacity pistol. While the shooter is not consciously counting rounds as they are fired, an automatic counter engages in the shooter's brain and allows for reloading at the right time.

The experienced shooter is also able to feel the slide shut on an empty chamber, whether from shooting the pistol dry without an active last-shot lock-open feature or because a magazine wasn't properly seated, thus allowing the slide to close and not chamber a round. (A difference in the sound of the slide's operation can also be detected by the experienced shooter.) All of these factors are good incentive for a shooter to practice with one pistol and one type of magazine and with the same technique every time. (An experienced shooter's automatic round counter is thrown off when using pistols of various capacities. This also holds true for shooters who interchange magazine capacities in the single-stack autopistol. I recommend selecting the best magazine—function and capacity-wise— and using it exclusively in all training. This will help you develop a reliable automatic round counter.

The speed reload. Note that two cartridge cases are still high in the air as the empty magazine is ejected and the fresh one is brought into position.

Shooters who choose high-capacity pistols have a more difficult time maintaining a precise automatic count, but they do have a larger margin of error because of the increased capacity. Mechanical round counters have been incorporated into some pistol stocks, but they are unnecessary and are not a substitute for proper shooter skills.)

Which Thumb?

Shooters who use a 1911 with a functional last-shot lock-open feature and who have fired their pistol dry will find that the thumb of the support hand is a much superior digit to release the slide than is the thumb of the strong hand, because the support-hand thumb is already in the area of the slide stop after it seats the fresh magazine and rolls back into firing position. Releasing the slide stop with the weak-hand thumb allows the shooter to resume firing as soon as the slide returns forward because the strong hand is already in a complete firing position. Also, shooters who use the strong-hand thumb to release the slide stop often find that they need to shift their grip to use the strong-hand thumb or have an extended slide release lever installed, both of which are less than good ideas because shifting the strong-hand grip on the pistol increases the time it takes to resume firing, and an extended slide release lever can cause problems in reliability and holstering of the pistol.

How Fast Is Fast?

An experienced, single-stack 1911 shooter can fire, reload, and continue firing with almost no break in the firing action. The proficient shooter/reloader can typically accomplish a reload in approximately one second, and even moderately proficient 1911 shooters can complete a reload in about two seconds. Muscle memory developed from serious practice should allow reloading to become a natural part of the firing process. Once this skill is developed, shooters feel less inclined to opt for the poorer handling features of the wide, high-capacity autopistols.

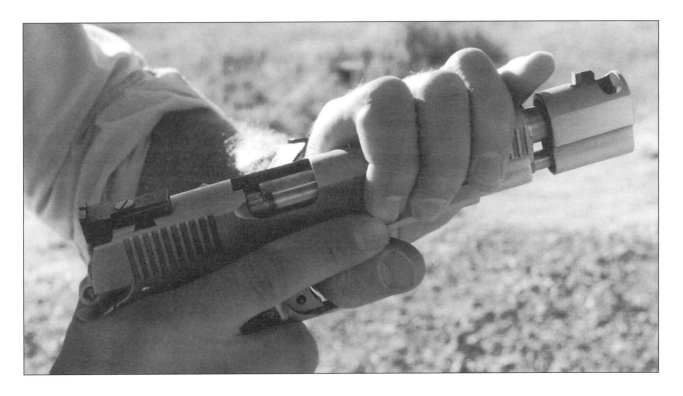

The press check.

Use the weak-hand thumb when releasing the slide.

The Mechanics and Finer Points Of Reloading

Make sure you have another magazine to load before ejecting the one in the pistol. You may need the last round or two in the ejected magazine if you discover you have lost or forgotten your extra magazines. Also, some pistols other than the 1911, such as the Browning Hi-Power, won't fire without a magazine seated. If there is no extra magazine available, there is no sense in speed ejecting the magazine onto the ground and risking contamination.

When seating a magazine, it should be firmly positioned but not hammered into the pistol. Hammering in the magazine is commonly done by inexperienced shooters and in Hollywood portrayals of pistol reloading. It is unnecessary and can be counterproductive. The magazine should be seated consistently and the magazine itself should allow for such consistency. Note, however, that a fully loaded eight- or ten-round magazine may require a substantial impact on the base to lock it in the pistol if the slide is forward, but the same fully loaded magazine will easily lock into place in a pistol that has the slide locked to the rear. This makes for inconsistent seating. The properly designed seven-round magazine gives a similar seating feel whether the slide is forward or locked to the rear. This consistency is very important when operating at high speed, because inconsistency can cause the shooter to slow down, hesitate, or be rough when reloading.

Improper seating of poor quality magazines can cause problems. Magazines with welded floor plates can fracture during regular hard seating of the magazines, which results in the cartridges and magazine spring being ejected through the bottom of the pistol after the magazine floor plate gives way. Slamming a poor quality magazine into place with the slide locked to the rear can also cause the top round in the magazine to spread the feed lips to the point that the magazine becomes wedged in the pistol, and the slide may not go forward, either. This is a difficult stoppage to clear in a hurry, one that could be completely avoided by using proper technique and quality magazines.

The speed load is the applicable course of action when you have run your pistol empty or nearly empty in an emergency situation. Cover should be used whenever possible. If the pistol has been fired substantially and is very dirty or otherwise contaminated, you may find that moving the pistol using a flicking motion can speed magazine ejection from a contaminated magazine well, but if the contamination is serious, the magazine may have to be manually removed. Under normal conditions with a relatively clean pistol, all magazines you use for duty carry should fall free under their own weight, even when empty. This is an important factor in speed reloading.

The follower design in the magazine you use is critical. The seven-round #47 W-R magazine incorporates a two-legged follower design that keeps the cartridges at a proper feed angle from the first shot to the last, and it gives positive slide stop operation. Shortened followers, in many cases made to accommodate an eighth round in a seven-round magazine, can be inconsistent in feed angle, reliability, and slide stop operation. Magazines that cause the pistol to operate inconsistently should not be used. Some split-lipped follower designs will activate the slide lock on some occasions and slip past the slide lock on others, thus allowing the slide to close on an empty chamber and the magazine to become somewhat locked in the gun. This abnormal operation requires additional shooter concentration to bring the gun back into firing condition.

Quality stainless steel magazines reduce the possibility of contamination when they hit the ground. During heavy range practice and training sessions where conditions permit, a ground tarp can ease wear and tear on magazines as well as make brass collection easier.

When loading a magazine, always hold the magazine in your weak hand and push down on the top round or magazine follower before inserting the next round. This takes the pressure off of the magazine lips and avoids stressing them.

Magazines subjected to heavy use, especially in the area of speed reloading, should be well examined for bent or cracked lips prior to being put back on duty status. This is very important to do when range personnel are following behind the shooter and the possibility of several people stepping on the magazines exists. Always follow magazine maintenance guidelines.

Overseating

Shooters who carry the Officers model as a backup weapon to a full-size Government model should be aware that the full-size Government model magazine will fit and function in the Officers model. A problem can occur if the Officers model is fired dry, the slide locks open, and the longer Government model magazine is overseated, which won't allow the slide to return forward. When the slide is forward the longer magazine can be firmly seated normally and not be accidently overseated. However, a problem can arise if the shooter is firing over cover or from a prone position with the bottom of the extended magazine in contact with a hard surface. During slide function, the slide moves to the rear, and the downward pressure of the pistol onto the hard surface can drive the magazine deeper into the pistol while the slide is to the rear, which interferes with the slide returning to battery. There are extended magazines for the Officers model that have stops on the front of the magazine which prevent overseating, although these prevent the use of the longer magazine in the Government model. Also, using the extended magazine in the Officers model reduces its concealability. A shooter who carries an Officers model with the extended magazine protruding from the butt would be better served by a full-size Government model's better handling qualities and still have nearly the same concealability.

Dedicated Officers model magazines are now available from Wilson's Pistol Products. A six-round and a seven-round version were originally

The tactical reload.

available, but the six-round version, which I preferred, has now been discontinued. Although most shooters obviously prefer the increased capacity, many overlook the importance of magazine seating consistency and two-legged follower reliability. This can still be achieved with the seven-round magazine by installing a two-legged follower and loading the magazine with six rounds.

Remember, don't practice with cheap magazines and use quality magazines on duty; continuity is everything. Occasional damage and replacement of quality magazines should be considered as a required expense in maintaining and training with your complete carry system. Preventive maintenance and detailed inspection of your magazines will eliminate the possibility of a training-damaged magazine or a weak magazine spring making it into service in your street carry system.

TACTICAL RELOADING

The number of rounds expended by a proficient shooter in a close-range, self-defense encounter is likely to be quite limited. This leaves the shooter's pistol in a condition of being only slightly downloaded. An experienced shooter should be able to smoothly and quickly top off his weapon while retaining the partially loaded magazine for possible future use. This will also bring his pistol back up to full capacity in case the encounter continues. This is commonly called the tactical reload.

To perform the tactical reload, obtain a fresh magazine from your magazine pouch with your weak hand, bring it to the strong-hand hold, and drop the partially loaded magazine from your pistol into the palm of your weak hand and retain it there while seating the fresh magazine. (Put the partially loaded magazine where you know it will be available for later use if necessary. I don't recommend placing the partially loaded magazine back into the magazine pouch along with other fully loaded magazines because it would be easy to later confuse it for a fully loaded magazine on a speed reload.) The shooter should not only locate and acquire the fresh magazine, but bring it all the way to the pistol before ejecting the partially loaded magazine. This allows the fresh magazine to be in close proximity to the magazine well before the other is ejected and allows the pistol's readiness to remain in the highest condition possible during the loading sequence.

The speed and tactical reloads have merit and every defensive shooter should know how to perform them properly. Once they have been mastered, there will be little chance of the proficient shooter being caught with an empty pistol.

POSITION SHOOTING

Position shooting is extremely important for the practical defensive handgunner, not only for added accuracy in delivering his shots, but for protection from incoming fire. With dedicated practice the shooter can assume various shooting positions very quickly. Offhand, kneeling, and prone are probably the most popular, and on some occasions the sitting position is useful.

Weaver
For relatively close range combat shooting, the Weaver offhand position is probably the fastest for the experienced shooter because it is an almost natural standing position, very similar to an interview stance.

Naturally, offhand practical shooting stances are less stable than positions incorporating solid support. If the distance and target size dictate that a more supportive position is required, take a second longer and get into a supported position. By acquiring a proper supported position you increase your accuracy and become a smaller target yourself.

The standard and modified sitting positions.

Kneeling Weaver and Kneeling Isosceles

The kneeling position can be gotten in and out of very quickly, which can be very important. It is a reasonably stable position and lowers your profile. However, you must consider that many inexperienced or stressed shooters pull their shots low. This is also a good reason to attach a groin guard to your ballistic vest. This position is often good when using cover.

All of the basic positions allow almost the same grip and arm position as the standing modified Weaver stance, the only difference being body position. This makes position shooting quite consistent and relatively easy to learn. The kneeling position is quite functional if you keep the weak-side foot pointing at the target, put the strong-side knee on the ground, and sit back on the strong-side foot. The Weaver position can be used with the arms and upper body, and support can be gained by resting the weak-arm triceps on the weak-side knee. It is important to remember not to try and rest the weak-side elbow directly on the weak-side knee, which leads to an unstable position because of the shape of the joints.

Isosceles shooters in competition matches often place both knees on the ground with the upper body remaining locked in an isosceles position. While this technique has proven quite functional when employed by experienced competition shooters, the defensive shooter should consider the position's physical defensibility, as it may be somewhat slower to react from and move out of.

Some shooters find that maintaining their upper body in an offhand-like position allows for consistency, and some people have difficulty bending into a position that allows the weak-side arm to gain support from the weak-side leg. Comfort is an important consideration in position shooting performance. Evaluate these kneeling positions thoroughly and determine which delivers the best performance for you.

Sitting

The standard sitting position is cursed by some and adored by others. It is, however, not the most stable or comfortable because it can be slow to get into and difficult to move out of quickly.

A modified sitting position with the pistol braced between the knees is better. This modified position

is most common in long-distance pistol shooting, but could, in certain situations, be of use to the combat shooter. However, you must be aware that this position doesn't make effective use of your ballistic vest and makes you vulnerable to ricochets. Also, a shooter comfortable with this position could use it if knocked on his back and required to shoot between his knees. The shooter must clear the front of his knees with the muzzle and ensure that he doesn't interfere with slide operation or brass ejection from the pistol. Using a revolver in this position may present the shooter with the additional concern of minimizing the effect of side flash emitted from the barrel/cylinder gap.

Practice of this technique will allow the shooter to develop the necessary movement to smoothly get out of the position and return to his feet without any muzzle control problems.

Prone

The prone position is probably the most accurate, and an experienced shooter can assume it quite quickly. It can make the defensive shooter a very small target and help him make excellent use of cover. Shooters in the prone (or other positions on a hard surface) must be aware of the potential for incoming bullets to skip into their position. Remember that proper cover is that which stops bullets. (Concealment merely obscures the shooter from sight.)

The basic prone position is most quickly assumed by drawing the pistol first, bending at the waist, putting the palm of the weak hand on the ground in front of the shooter, and kicking both feet to the rear to land without injury. This method is quite fast, although its application may depend on the ground surface's potential to make more noise than preferred or injure the shooter. Loose debris on the deck could also attach itself to the shooter's

Getting into the prone position.

weak hand and interfere with the weak hand's supported position in the firing grip.

A more reserved and slower method of acquiring the prone position is to simply kneel on both knees before descending to the prone position with the arms and hands already locked into a firing grip. The slower descent minimizes the chance for injury and assures that no foreign material comes in between the two hands forming the firing grip. The forward fall can be regulated by the elbows.

The hands should come together in a shooting grip with the bottom edge of the support hand resting on the ground, not the butt of the

The prone position you select should be determined by the situation.

pistol. This is especially important when using an extended magazine without an insertion stop that can dig into the ground and cause a malfunction.

Ideally, the shooter's body should be at a 45-degree angle toward the weak side, the weak-side foot should be bent onto the back of the strong-side knee, and the upper torso should be rolled slightly onto the strong side, thus allowing the shooter to breathe easy without the resistance of lying on his chest. However, sometimes the 45-degree position is not the best for use of cover and must be adjusted accordingly. A straight-on prone position can work very well in some situations, too. Practice and experiment.

The shooter can elevate his shots in the prone position by rolling the support hand down and under the firing hand.

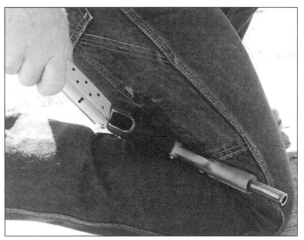

The behind-the-knee reload.

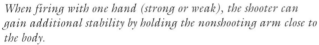

When firing with one hand (strong or weak), the shooter can gain additional stability by holding the nonshooting arm close to the body.

If you expect to be firing numerous rounds from the prone position and have advance warning of doing so, you may want to take a couple of magazines from their pouches and have them near your firing grip position. This allows for easier reloading and reduces movement. The ground conditions under your firing grip and equipment must be taken into consideration *before* you get into position.

There are a variety of methods you can use to elevate your prone firing grip, one of which is to simply elevate the entire firing grip while maintaining elbow contact with the ground. This, however, is not the preferred method, because it is less stable and allows for more muzzle flip. A preferred method is to maintain direct hand contact with the ground. The elevation required to make the shot, as well as the ground conditions, will determine how this will be best achieved. In most cases, on fairly level ground while shooting at a target of reasonable height, the shooter can simply hold his support-hand grip lower on the strong hand. This maintains contact between the two hands and keeps the support hand in contact with the ground while elevating the pistol. Again, experimentation will be necessary to determine which technique works best.

One-Hand Operation

A defensive shooter must also know how to shoot well with one hand, a skill that could be invaluable should one of your arms become disabled or restrained in a confrontation. Practice everything one-handed, including the draw, malfunction clearance, and the reload. This is another area where the autopistol is more operator friendly than the revolver.

One-handed firing is done by using the same basic handgun shooting skills discussed in Chapter 6, even though it is often more difficult. Also remember that one-handed firing generates a different felt recoil than two-handed pistol firing, so the pistol may feel as if it is torquing to one side. A substantial amount of one-handed and weak-handed firing is necessary to achieve relatively accurate hits at distances beyond point-blank range and not be surprised by the different feel of firing one-handed.

An adjustment in stance and arm position may be required to compensate for the difference between two- and one-handed firing. Try stepping forward with the firing-side foot and moving the shoulder of the firing hand forward and firmly holding it into a forward position to absorb recoil and thus aide in quicker sight recovery, especially when firing a full-powered pistol. A substantial amount of training and practice will be required to become proficient in one-handed shooting. This is an area that must not be overlooked by the defensive shooter.

If you are operating a single-action 1911 with a single-sided manual thumb safety, you must learn to operate it properly with either hand. This is not at all difficult when using the proper technique. It will, of course, require some safe practice.

Disengaging the single manual thumb safety with the weak hand merely requires the shooter to shift his grip, move the manual safety to the off position with the weak-hand thumb or rear portion of the weak-hand trigger finger, reposition his hand, and continue firing. The weak- or one-handed reload can easily be accomplished by holding the safe condition pistol in any safe position that facilitates the insertion of a fresh magazine with the uninjured hand, such as holding the pistol between the knees, in the joint of the knee, or on a firm surface.

Dropping the spent magazine from the pistol should be no problem with either hand. A shooter can operate the magazine release button with the right-hand thumb when the pistol is held in his right hand. When the pistol is held in his left hand, using the left-hand index finger is best. (Shooters who complain that standard Government model magazine catch spring tension is too strong for them to easily operate the magazine release button should work on hand strength exercises rather than replace the magazine catch lock spring with a lighter tension spring. A lighter tension spring could allow the magazine button to be unintentionally depressed and release the magazine.)

A variety of one-handed slide-racking techniques are available. A round can be chambered from the magazine of a 1911 Government model without a full-length guide rod by pushing the front underside of the slide against a hard object until it moves back to the point where the frame's dust cover stops the slide's rearward travel. At this point the slide will be sufficiently back to pick up the top round in the magazine and chamber it properly, provided the slide is allowed to return forward briskly.

Many modern 1911s feature a one-piece guide rod, so alternative methods must be available. One of the most popular methods for use with a behind-the-knee magazine reload is to position the front top of the slide area on the back of a hard-soled

The one-handed heel charge.

The tap, rack, and fire drill.

shoe or boot and briskly press forward and allow the slide to chamber the top round in the magazine. If the slide is properly positioned on the boot's heel, all the pressure will be directed at the top front of the slide just above the barrel. A ruggedly installed front sight will also absorb this slide racking pressure, but the preferred area of forced application is the front upper side of the slide, just above the barrel. Racking the slide this way allows the barrel to extend out the front of the slide and away from the shooter. However, you must be aware of your background. This is a safe and effective method provided it is done properly.

A rugged, fixed rear sight may also provide a surface for racking the slide with one hand. Conversely, adjustable sights with a separate leaf attached to the rear sight may provide a surface area conducive to hooking on a solid object, but may not provide the long-term durability to use this option. A sight without this durability could be broken and leave the shooter with no rear sight notch.

Other rear sights, fixed or adjustable, may be so streamlined in their design (to avoid sharp edges and snagging for concealed carry application) that they don't have sufficient area for hooking onto a solid object to rack the slide. Such pistols are best suited for one-handed slide racking by using the front top portion of the slide or breech face. Depending on what solid objects are available to hook the slide on, the top of the breech face just above the barrel hood may provide a sufficient shelf from which to operate the slide.

Poor quality magazines wedged in the pistol can complicate one-handed reloads even further. Another very good reason to use only the best magazines.

Logic dictates that if the slide can be racked to chamber a round by using these techniques, it is also possible to unchamber a live round in the same way. The installation of a full-length guide rod and the activation of the manual thumb safety makes this extremely unlikely. The mere possibility of it happening in a fast-paced encounter should make you aware of the need to check the chamber whenever possible.

Problems

Other factors can affect your slide's operation. One is allowing the slide to become stopped or retarded by cover. This is possible when firing from vehicle ports or between the door post and the open door of an automobile and especially when firing from the spotlight cutout. Provided the shooter has a good sight picture, the sights should be clear of all obstructions (at least initially). Muzzle flip can cause the front sight to hook on the top of the firing port and cause a stoppage. (As discussed earlier, the heat of the encounter may draw the shooter's eye toward the threat rather than the sights. This could cause the shooter to begin firing with the rear of the front sight hooked around the front of the cover he is using. In this case the slide may short stroke or prevent function altogether. A distracted shooter in this situation may not notice the condition of his pistol or realize that the empty case of the first fired round has not been ejected. This can cause serious lag time in the event the shooter tries to fire again. Remember to *tap*, *rack*, and *fire* in this instance.)

A second area where slide interference can result in a malfunction is firearm take-away. If two people are grappling for the pistol and it discharges when one or both of them have a solid grip on the gun, it may discharge once and not cycle. In the heat of the confrontation, the operator may not realize what has happened, and the operator may experience a failure to fire when he tries to take a follow-up shot.

Training courses that require the shooter to engage targets at various distances, heights, and directions are good training in reactionary turning.

Defensive shooters must always be aware of potential interference with slide operation and confirm the chamber's condition as soon as the opportunity presents itself. A chamber observation port cut into the barrel hood allows the shooter to observe the brass case, but is that round live or expended? If you suspect slide interference when a shot was fired, tap the magazine and rack the slide immediately. If time permits, carefully check the chamber to determine if the round is live or expended. This way you will possibly be able to avoid jacking out a live round.

TACTICS

An experienced defensive shooter should be able to move quietly in a constant state of readiness.

Forward Movement

One movement method that works well is maintaining the pistol in a two-handed low ready position with the thumbs on top of the engaged manual thumb safety and moving using a silent shuffling of the feet—taking approximately eight- to ten-inch steps and being careful to stay balanced and never crossing your feet. This is a slow, quiet method of moving that allows you to remain in a solid firing position at all times, although the speed the method uses may be too slow for some situations. The right shoes or boots make being quiet easier, too.

Moving quickly while maintaining the ability to fire at any time, including on the move, can be accomplished by the well-trained shooter. A good technique is to maintain your upper body in a firing position compatible with the situation; the lower portion of your body can be positioned and moved in what is known as the "Groucho" walk, but you will have to determine what variation serves you best.

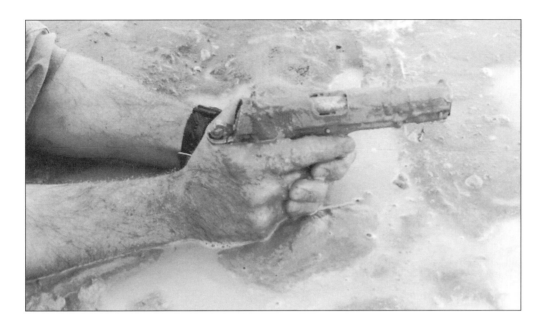

Shooting during inclement weather must be part of your training program.

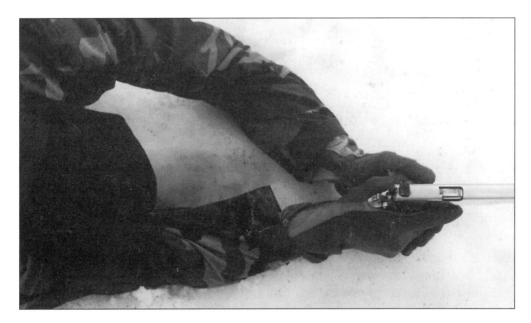

The effectiveness of the technique is in the bent knees acting as shock absorbers, which allows the legs to take up any unevenness in the ground surface and maintain the upper body in a relatively stable, ready-to-fire position.

The technique can be used at different speeds, depending on the skill of the operator and the situation. In some situations, the unexpected aggressive forward action and accurate shooting on the move by the operator may be so disconcerting to the assailant that he will be unable to deal with his opponent.

Backward Movement

Shooting during slow, moderate, and charging advances should be skills acquired by the defensive shooter, and shooting while walking backward should also be feasible. If your attacker is relatively inexperienced and using point shooting methods, his accuracy will diminish substantially past point-blank ranges, whereas your highly proficient shooting skills will be sufficient to deliver accurate rounds at more extended distances. Backing away from the fight can also be a positive factor in a later court proceeding.

Turning

Safe, reliable turning techniques should also be a part of the defensive shooter's repertoire, especially when surprises are possible.

Left Turn

The left turn (by the right-handed shooter) is best accomplished by taking a step to the left with the left leg and pointing the left foot toward the threat area. The right foot pivots into alignment with the left foot and the shooter acquires a balanced Weaver stance. During this movement the pistol is drawn in its normal fashion and brought to bear.

Right Turn

The right turn is best accomplished by stepping toward the target with the left foot and pointing it in the direction of the target. The right foot then pivots and comes into alignment with the left foot. The draw is accomplished as normal and the pistol is brought to bear.

180-Degree Turn

The 180-degree turn can be performed by stepping back (toward the target), pivoting, and bringing the pistol to bear. I don't like this method because it can put you substantially closer to an assailant who might be partially or completely obscured, and you could easily get off balance if suddenly charged or otherwise engaged by the assailant. Stepping toward the threat also puts you closer to any weapon the assailant may produce.

Transitioning from the high-intensity hand-held light to the gun-mounted light can be swift and smooth. Be sure to keep the hand-held light well in front of you so that you don't illuminate what your strong hand is doing. Also, never perform an initial search with the gun-mounted light, as you could inadvertently cover a nonthreatening person with your gun.

I prefer the step-away-and-turn method, which is quite simple if the shooter doesn't allow his thought process to make it complicated; just do it naturally. Step forward (away from the target area) one full step with the right foot. Pivot on the ball of the right foot as soon as it touches the ground and move the left foot over. This places your feet in a Weaver-style stance. Upon completion of the turn, the left foot will be the lead foot. The left foot can be brought back slightly into a more secure Weaver stance if necessary, or you may continue to shuffle rearward away from the threat area while covering the situation with your 1911.

Weather

Serious defensive shooters expose themselves to inclement weather training, including gloved operation of the 1911. Whereas some shooters use a fingerless glove to ensure undisturbed finger contact with the controls of a pistol, in severe winter weather exposed fingers can quickly become numb to the point that fine motor skills and normal feel of the fingers are diminished. For this reason, fully gloved handgun operation should be experienced.

This is an area that demonstrates the needed difference between a competition-only trigger and a practical street-carry trigger. An extremely light competition trigger presents feel problems for the shooter operating with a gloved trigger finger or numb fingers. Frigid weather conditions also help to demonstrate the superiority of a more powerful trigger resetting action in the autopistol. Triggers with light resets may work fine in clean summer conditions, but often cause problems in dirty or extremely cold environments.

Low Light

Target identification and illumination can be a critical element in the final outcome of a high-stress encounter. Whether you choose to employ night firing for sight alignment (which isn't recommended) or tritium night sight inserts, you must be familiar with their operation under realistic conditions. The shooter who objectively evaluates the performance differences between the two will certainly opt for the tritium inserts.

Flashlight shooting techniques should be evaluated and, once settled upon, should be an area of dedicated practice. Experimentation between the syringe operation of a small combat light, the

Clearing a stovepipe stoppage.

techniques common to a full-size patrol light, and the magazine-mounted light should all be tested. Dedicated practice in all of these areas will allow the shooter to operate effectively under nearly all conditions.

MALFUNCTIONS

There is a cause and cure for every malfunction, so a shooter with a malfunctioning autopistol shouldn't decide that he has to put up with unreliability because he is shooting an auto. The claims about autopistols being unreliable and inaccurate have been disproved so many times that it is not worth dedicating another section to the topic. Suffice it to say that any logical person could easily surmise that the top shooters in the world certainly wouldn't shoot an unreliable pistol for a living, nor would professional defensive pistol instructors. It is important to note, however, that the chosen pistol of a professional is tuned and tested for reliability and accuracy, rather than blindly trusted.

If your "out of the box" mass-produced 1911 is malfunctioning, which is somewhat common, the required basic reliability modifications should be made to it by a dedicated pistolsmith before it is used for street carry. Consider, however, that if your pistol is properly modified but is encountering some stoppages, it could simply be out of adjustment, the ammunition could be at fault, the magazines may be problematic, or the shooter could be at fault. A shooter who abuses his pistol by improper or infrequent cleaning, snapping his extractor over chambered rounds, or slamming the slide on an empty chamber can expect malfunctions or other problems to eventually develop. The 1911 is extremely durable and reliable when properly set up, but there is no reason to abuse the pistol. Abuse is the mark of an amateur.

In any event, proper diagnosis and modification of your pistol will correct any minor reliability problems. If you are having such problems, have them immediately cured by a professional. In the event that your pistol was improperly modified to the point that a major component of the pistol has been altered beyond repair, the solution may be best achieved by starting the process over with a new base firearm and ensuring that the work is done properly the first time.

The shooter should keep in mind, however, that while a handgun can be brought to a level of outstanding reliability, it is still a mechanical tool. As is the case with any mechanical item, the potential for parts breakage or unexpected stoppage is always present. In the event that you are affected by such a problem, it is likely to occur at the worst possible time. In this event, or if your primary weapon is lost or taken away, a concealed yet accessible backup that is compatible with your primary ammunition and magazine is often your best solution. This is like carrying a spare tire for your automobile or taking two vehicles into the backcountry.

Clearing a minor stoppage of the 1911 is usually a simple and quick procedure when performed by a knowledgeable shooter, but you must be aware of the correct stoppage clearance drill for each type of malfunction.

Failure To Fire

When the pistol fails to fire, or fires only one round and then fails to fire the next, the problem is very likely an incorrectly seated magazine. Two typical problems are:

- The shooter inserted a loaded magazine and operated the slide without the magazine being fully seated, resulting in the top round not being chambered when the slide went forward. If the shooter then holstered the weapon without first checking the chamber and magazine seating, he wouldn't know whether a round was chambered. The shooter should check the chamber for a live round and the magazine for proper seating every time the weapon is loaded.
- The shooter inserted a magazine, seated it properly, chambered a round, removed the magazine, placed one more round in the magazine, and then reinserted the magazine without fully seating it, resulting in a failure to fire on the second shot. This is why it is so important to have base pads installed on all your magazines to help ensure that the magazine locks into place properly.

The cure for most failure-to-fire malfunctions is tapping the bottom of the magazine with the palm of the support hand, seating it properly, racking the slide, and then continuing to fire if necessary, unless of course the magazine falls completely out of the pistol when it is drawn, in which case a fresh magazine would have to be installed and the slide racked. (If the dropped magazine is retrieved and time permits, don't forget to inspect it for dirt and damage before using it.)

Failure To Eject

Another type of stoppage is failure to eject, such as a vertical empty case getting stuck in the ejection port, which is commonly called a stovepipe or a smokestack. This type of stoppage could be caused by an improperly modified or adjusted pistol, improper ammunition being fired for the spring weight installed in the pistol, or shooter error.

A simple solution for less experienced shooters is to just clear and reload the pistol: lock the slide to the rear, hit the magazine eject button, ensure that the empty case and any partially chambered rounds have fallen free, insert a fresh magazine, and release the slide. A more experienced shooter will be able to diagnose the situation more accurately and perform a stoppage clearance drill that allows retention of the ammunition in the pistol.

The shooter will most likely see the brass case interfering with his sight picture as it protrudes directly up from the ejection port area and blocks his view of the front sight. The shooter must first determine if there is another live cartridge in place in the breech face and partially in the chamber. If so, all that is required is removal of the empty case, which can be done by grabbing the case, although it will possibly be hot, between the thumb and the forefinger and pulling it free, thus allowing the slide to go forward to completely chamber the next round. At this point the pistol is operational again. Recommendations of karate chopping or otherwise hitting the case with your hand are foolish, often ineffective, and can injure your hand. Don't needlessly complicate things. If you can't simply pull the case from the port because it is down too low, slightly retract the slide and flick the pistol to the side. Let the case fall out and let the slide chamber the next round.

A high stovepipe can also be brushed against a solid object, which doesn't require the shooter to change his firing grip.

If the stovepipe is protruding from the ejection port but the next cartridge has not been picked up by the slide, you will be required to not only remove the spent case, but also to retract the slide enough to pick up the next round in the magazine. This can be accomplished by ensuring that the magazine is seated, grasping the stovepiped case and the slide with the weak hand, and retracting the slide to allow lifting the spent case out of the port area. The slide can then be allowed to return forward after full retraction and chamber the next round. This clearance can also be accomplished without changing the firing grip on the pistol by simply brushing the stovepiped case against a solid object to dislodge it and then performing a one-handed cycle of the slide.

Failure To Feed

Failure to feed is another stoppage. If a round that has stopped in the feedway is not severely lodged, it can usually be helped into the chamber by rapping on the bottom of the magazine, thus bumping it up the feed ramp and into the chamber. If the rap on the bottom of the magazine doesn't work, the follow-up racking of the slide normally will.

If the secondary slide racking doesn't chamber the cartridge, there is a good possibility that the cartridge has experienced some bullet setback. The best solution to this stoppage is to simply reload. Lock the slide to the rear and depress the magazine ejection button. There is a good possibility the magazine won't be ejected because of the top round in the magazine having moved forward. The magazine should be stripped from the pistol by grabbing the base pad or applying downward pressure on the magazine (through the ejection port). This should clear the magazine and the stopped cartridge and allow for insertion of a fresh magazine and chambering of the next round.

Failure To Extract

Failure to extract is probably the most severe of the basic stoppages because it can take some time to clear. A failure to extract is oftentimes the result of a very dirty chamber or an improperly adjusted or broken extractor, the latter of which happens because someone has been snapping the extractor over rounds that were individually inserted into the chamber, or because someone was practicing extraction clearance drills improperly. If you abuse your pistol in this way, you can break your extractor hook and turn your pistol into a slow-shooting single-shot. Although substantial advancements have been made in the development of superior quality extractors that can withstand substantial abuse, there is no need to subject them to improper operating techniques.

When you fire a round and it fails to extract, the slide still moves to the rear and picks up a fresh round from the magazine. The slide then tries to chamber the fresh round behind the empty case left in the chamber. This condition can be quite confusing to people who don't study serious pistolcraft, but to the knowledgeable shooter it is a relatively simple malfunction to clear. Lock the slide open, hit the magazine ejection button, rake or pull the magazine out of the pistol, shake or extract the fired case out of the pistol, and reload. This is commonly referred to as lock, drop, rake, shake, and reload. A potential problem in this clearance drill is the spent case in the chamber. If the chamber is clean, it may allow the empty case to fall out of the chamber when the pistol is angled up and shaken. If so, this portion of the problem is cured. If the case does not shake out, you will either have to poke it out with a range rod or pen (during range practice), or run the extractor over the stuck case (in an emergency situation), hopefully fully extracting and ejecting it.

If you can avoid running your extractor over the cartridge case lip, do so. In an emergency situation where you need the pistol cleared fast, you might have to do it and hope for the best. If you do it and completely break your extractor hook, it will complicate problems even more and turn your auto into a single-shot. Some shooting instructors with very limited knowledge of the 1911 submit this problem to their students for practice on a regular basis. Some of these same instructors put single rounds into the chamber of the pistol and snap the slide over the chambered round. In doing this, the possibility of snapping the extractor hook and the probability of disrupting the extractor tension exists.

After this improper procedure is done a number of times, the extractor hook can be broken or get so far out of adjustment that future malfunctions are a certainty. Many pistols have had to be adjusted after instructors demanded that this procedure be completed. What's worse is that some pistol owners don't realize the potential for damage and future malfunction and continue to carry the pistol after the training session.

Instructors who recommend or require that this clearance drill be performed on a regular basis obviously do not know how the 1911 is designed to operate. During the feeding cycle of the 1911, cartridges slide under the extractor hook, which is not designed to pivot and snap over cartridges being fed into the chamber. Therefore, this drill should be used only in an emergency. If you've had to do it, done it by accident, or have been doing it because of misunderstanding, have your pistol checked by a competent pistolsmith as soon as possible.

Slide-Stop Malfunctions

Your 1911's operation can sometimes be interrupted by the slide stop unexpectedly activating, causing the slide to lock open while live cartridges are in the pistol. This problem can be avoided by deactivating the last-shot lock-open feature. The possibility of any slide stop failure can be greatly minimized by replacing the factory slide stop with one specially designed and made of heat-treated steel. Plus, the possibility of the slide stop being inadvertently pushed out of position in the frame can be eliminated by milling the slide stop crosspin flush with the right side of the frame.

False locking is more of a problem with high-capacity pistols than with single stacks, although it can occur with a single stack for a variety of reasons. Misdiagnosis and doing more than is necessary only adds to the problem. False locking is best cured by the proper fitting of a correct slide stop or the total elimination of the lock feature. The cylinder of a revolver does not lock open after the last shot and knowledgeable operators apply their skill to keep the gun loaded. The same can be done with the 1911, provided the operator is skilled and does not need a mechanical reminder to load his pistol. To clear this stoppage, depress the slide stop and allow the slide to move forward and chamber the top round from the magazine.

Firing Pin Malfunctions

If a full-powered firing pin spring is used along with a properly fitted firing pin stop, a firing pin "stop drop" stoppage is very unlikely. When the firing pin stop drops out of its fully seated position in the slide, the bottom portion of the firing pin stop can catch on the hammer when the slide returns forward and stop the slide's forward movement. The simplest clearance procedure for this stoppage is to lock the slide open and push the firing pin stop back into position, thus allowing the slide to fully chamber the next round. A point of concern in this stoppage is the possibility of losing the firing pin stop or firing pin and spring if the shooter's hand is not carefully cupped over the rear of the slide. This is especially true with pre-Series 80 pistols that don't have the firing pin lock feature. The best solution is to prevent the problem with a properly fitted stop and spring before it occurs.

Final Cautionary Thoughts On Malfunctions

A word of caution when clearing malfunctions: don't beat or slam the slide around unnecessarily, especially with live ammunition in the pistol. A live round in the ejection port can cause serious injury.

Once you learn proper malfunction clearance procedures, malfunctions can be cleared very smoothly and rapidly. If you cannot identify the cause of a malfunction, have the pistol diagnosed and corrected by a competent smith before carrying the pistol. Out-of-spec reloaded ammo, bad magazines, and poor maintenance are usually operator-level items that can be checked. Your pistol should be completely reliable or not carried at all.

If learning and understanding specific clearances seems complicated or even overwhelming, get some competent instruction and practice more. If you still feel they may be a problem for you under pressure, you could condense nearly all of them down into one procedure: unload the pistol completely and then reload it. This does waste more time and ammo than proper procedures, but it is simple to remember: eject the magazine, rack the slide to clear the weapon, insert a fresh magazine, and rack the slide to chamber a round. It's a simple tactic that can be recalled even under stress.

Lastly, even though a modified pistol can be totally reliable for a substantial period of time, you must never become lax in your training and weapon maintenance, both of which will become quite important when Murphy's Law is applied in a defensive encounter.

KNIVES AS ADJUNCT WEAPONS TO THE 1911 AND OTHER HANDGUNS

Most people have heard the saying, "never bring a knife to a gunfight." When delivered as a line in an action movie, such a statement may have some entertainment value, but for today's professional who is armed with a 1911, it is a dangerous and misleading belief.

First of all, a fight is a fight. It is highly unlikely that you will receive an engraved invitation to a violent encounter, and it's even less likely that you will get a packing list specifying the most effective weapons to bring along besides your 1911. Close combat is very fluid and dynamic. There are no written rules, referees, or time limits. Therefore, a gunfight can become a knife fight, club fight, or wrestling match in the blink of an eye. When this change occurs, you must be prepared to adjust your tactics and choice of weapon instantly to adapt to the situation.

This concept is not at all new within the realm of firearms tactics. For example, if forced to take a shot at 100 yards, most people would naturally transition from the 1911 to a rifle or to a shotgun loaded with slugs. The same concept applies at contact distance when flailing limbs and flying punches make accurate shots with a 1911 difficult and potentially hazardous to you and innocent bystanders. In such circumstances, the best course of action might be to consciously select or transition to a more appropriate weapon, such as a knife. With this in mind, let's look at the qualities of edged weapons and how they can supplement the 1911.

One unique quality of the knife is that it allows an incremental application of force—you can actually select the amount of damage you're willing to inflict. On the low end, you can simply produce the knife to prevent an actual violent encounter. In this role, the knife can often be more effective than a gun. Because most people have cut themselves and seen others cut, they have an automatic understanding of the knife's capabilities. On the other hand, very few people have been shot. Therefore, despite the 1911's advantages in terms of power and distance, the understanding of the threat is not as automatic and may not be effective. Cutting a person also typically requires much less commitment than shooting him, potentially making the situation more real to the person facing it.

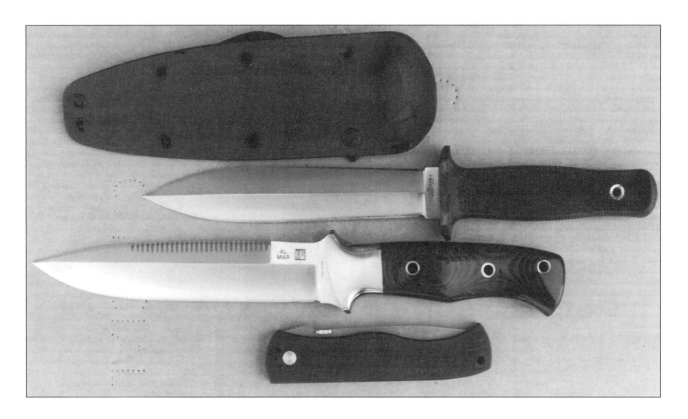

Substantial improvements in knife and sheath designs, including folding knives, have made knives excellent backups to the handgun.

Moving up the scale, the knife can be used as an impact weapon without bringing the blade into play. A closed folding knife held in the fist can be used to strike powerful blows to nerve centers and bony parts of the body, which could end a fight very quickly. The pommel or butt of a fixed blade knife can also be used in this manner without having to resort to using the blade.

Cutting is the next step up in the knife's scale of force. Generally less lethal than stabbing or puncturing wounds, a knife cut can still produce impressive bleeding, shock, and incapacitation. Knife cuts can also be selectively administered to further refine the scale of force. A cut to the hand is usually less severe and sends a different message than a cut to the body or face. Likewise, defensive cuts which intercept your attacker's incoming blows reflect a lower level of force than committed offensive cuts.

At the top of the knife's scale of force is thrusting. From both a practical and legal standpoint, thrusting is considered a determined application of lethal force. Puncture wounds are generally more serious than incised or cutting wounds and are more likely to produce immediate shock. They also generate more pain than cuts and thus are more effective fight stoppers.

With a knife, any of these levels of force can be selectively applied at any time during a conflict. From a tactical standpoint, this provides the defender with many more options than those offered by the 1911. Legally, this also makes claiming self-defense easier because restraint can be clearly proven. For example, if you cut your attacker, you can

Self-defense and weapons instructor Michael Janich demonstrating a knife throw with a transition to the handgun.

explain that this was done consciously in preference to stabbing him. Conversely, it's very difficult to shoot someone a little bit with a 1911.

Another feature of the knife is that it has limited range. On the positive side, this means there is no fear of missed or overpenetrative shots striking innocent parties downrange. On the down side, it also means that you must get much closer to your opponent to employ the knife. When comparing the knife to the 1911 directly, this is a definite disadvantage. In the context of this discussion, however, this limitation is actually irrelevant because the transition to the knife or decision to employ it in preference to the 1911 is being made consciously and is based on the tactical situation.

Perhaps the greatest advantages of the knife are that it is not subject to the limitations of ammunition supply and is much less prone to malfunction than the out-of-the-box 1911. In other words, you don't have to reload it and it's probably not going to break in the middle of a fight (given that you choose a knife appropriate for defensive use). Reliability is the quality valued above all others when it comes to weapon selection, and the knife certainly excels in this area. If your 1911 should malfunction or run dry in the middle of a fight, in many cases you are better off transitioning to another weapon than leaving yourself vulnerable while you attempt to clear or reload your pistol. This obviously depends entirely upon the tactical situation, but at close quarters, the immediate availability of a secondary weapon is a definite advantage.

Although many people who carry guns feel they are somehow immune to their weapons being taken from them, statistics concerning law enforcement officers shot with their own weapons should convince you that this is a definite possibility. In such scenarios, a knife can be an invaluable asset as a secondary weapon to either assist in retaining your firearm or to counterattack before your gun can be used against you.

Martial artist Erik Remmen of Northwest Safari has developed a weapon retention system based on carrying two small folding knives in addition to a sidearm. Remmen's course has found great favor with law enforcement personnel, and his methods have already saved the lives of a number of officers.

Another excellent reason to carry a knife as a secondary weapon is the lack of universal concealed carry laws. Although your position as a law enforcement officer or concealed carry permit holder may entitle you to carry a firearm in your jurisdiction or authorized area of carry, as soon as you set foot in another area, your right to carry may disappear. However, practically every jurisdiction allows the carry of some form of knife without a permit. By carrying and becoming familiar with the use of an edged weapon as a backup, you can again smoothly transition in response to the change in tactical, or in this case legal environments.

With all this said, I believe that the greatest advantage of carrying a knife and learning its proper use as a weapon is that it educates the individual concerning the true capabilities of that weapon. I first became interested in knife combatives when I was studying my first martial arts style. After diligently practicing a number of that style's defenses against knife attacks, I still felt unprepared to face a knife-wielding attacker. When I questioned my instructor about the apparent inefficiency of the techniques we were learning, he offered some sage advice: "If you want to learn how to defend against a weapon, first learn how to use that weapon. Then you'll understand its weaknesses and how to exploit them."

As basic as this may seem, it is a concept that is still grossly misunderstood by many people. Whenever I discuss knife fighting with gun owners, I get the same tired response: "If someone pulls a knife on me, I'll just shoot the SOB!" Curiously, most people who offer this opinion do not actually carry guns on a regular basis. Even if they did, they probably never trained to draw and fire quickly against an attacker rushing them with a knife. They also probably have never trained to respond to a knife attack with an unarmed defense or improvised weapon defense that would buy them time to draw and shoot. In short, these people are totally unaware of what a knife can do and how quickly and savagely it can do it. They assume that since the gun is technologically superior to the knife that it will automatically prevail against an attacker armed with a knife. To me, that amounts to a serious underestimation of a likely opponent and an easy way to end up in a body bag.

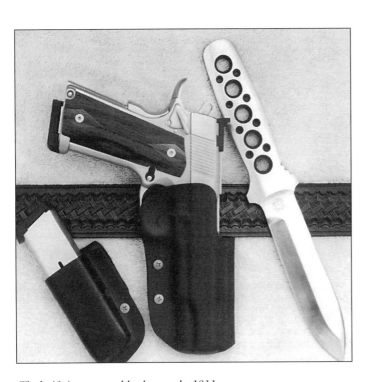

The knife is a natural backup to the 1911.

This brings up a very important point: if you do choose to carry a knife as a secondary weapon, learn how to use it as well as or better than your firearm. Seek out qualified instruction and practice your skills often. Otherwise, you'll be no better off with a knife than you were without one. In fact, you might be worse off in that the increase in confidence produced by carrying the knife is not matched by a true increase in your ability to defend yourself.

A good knife is an excellent addition to anyone's personal equipment and an ideal companion to the 1911. The skill to use that knife, however, is an even better addition because with it comes an understanding of the knife's true capabilities. When you know what you've got, you'll know how to use it best. You'll also know how to keep the other guy from using it on you.

—Michael D. Janich

Chapter 8

MAINTENANCE OF THE 1911

GENERAL DISASSEMBLY

Disassembly of the 1911 takes substantially longer to describe or read about than it takes the proficient 1911 owner to complete.

Remove the magazine by pushing the magazine catch on the left side of the receiver. With the magazine out, clear the chamber by retracting the slide and locking it to the rear. The live chambered cartridge should be ejected onto a padded area rather than into the shooter's hand because if the shooter fumbles the catch, the round can strike the ejector and discharge (this happens more often than one might think). Inspect the chamber to ensure it is empty. A standard five-inch Government model without a full-length guide rod can be disassembled by holding the pistol in the right hand with the right index finger on the end of the slide stop crosspin. Simply pull the slide to the rear enough to line up the slide stop with the small half-moon disassembly notch on the left side of the slide. Once aligned, push the slide stop crosspin slightly out of the frame, then regrip the slide by positioning the right hand with the web underneath the beavertail grip safety and the forefingers over the top of the slide. Now the operator can manipulate the slide while removing the slide stop completely from the frame. Once this is accomplished the entire barrel, slide, spring, plug, and spring guide can be removed from the front of the frame. The palm of the left hand should be securely cupped around the bottom of the slide as it is removed to prevent the captive recoil spring from flying free once it is removed from the frame's dust cover area. Now the slide and related components can be disassembled without the recoil spring's pressure acting upon them.

The five-inch 1911 with a full-length guide rod is best disassembled from the front of the pistol. The same magazine removal and chamber clearance procedures should be completed prior to working on the barrel bushing area.

Under field conditions, the base of a magazine can be used to depress the spring plug into the slide enough to turn the bushing clockwise until it stops. A plastic nonmarring bushing wrench will make this task even easier. Safety glasses should be worn during this procedure because the spring plug is under substantial pressure, and allowing the plug to escape can result not only in loss of the plug but a serious injury to the operator. The bushing wrench and the operator's finger should be maintained on the recoil spring plug to contain it during removal. After the spring pressure is relieved, the slide stop can be removed and the entire slide assembly removed from the frame.

Remove the recoil spring and spring plug. The spring on the guide rod should be turned in a clockwise direction while being pulled gently forward and off of the guide rod. Once the spring is removed, the guide rod can be removed from the rear and then the barrel bushing can be turned to free its locking notch and be removed from the front. A slide and barrel assembly containing a tightly fitted barrel bushing may allow for easier bushing removal if the barrel is pulled slightly forward and out of its lockup position. A bushing that is snugly fitted to the barrel will be in its tightest position when the bushing is encircling the slightly enlarged end of a match-grade barrel. The barrel can now be removed from the front of the slide. The barrel's swinging link should be in its forward position to allow clearance through the bottom front of the slide. A link can cause a binding if removal is attempted while its in an up and back position. This is as far as the average operator should disassemble the 1911 for general cleaning purposes.

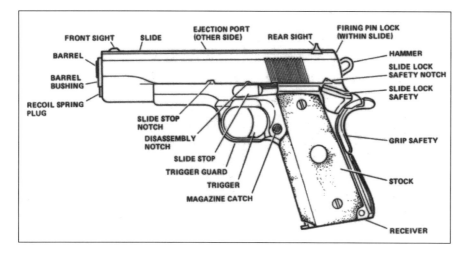

The Colt 1911.

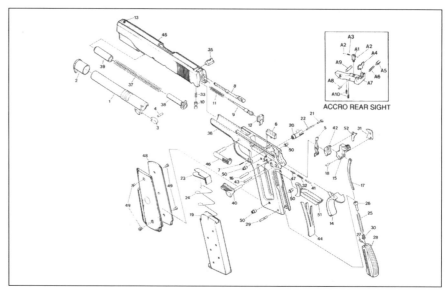

The 1911 exploded.

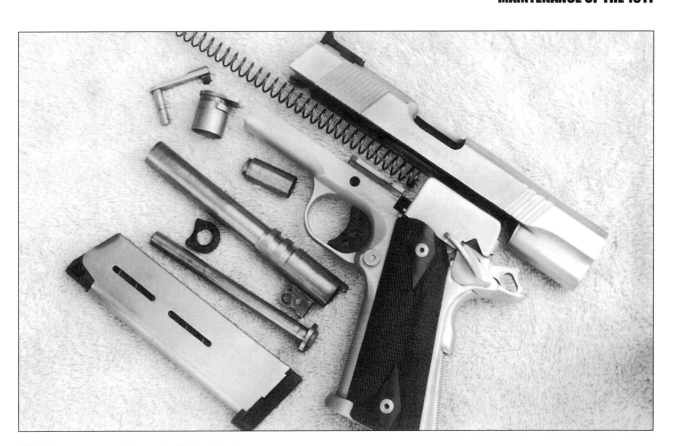

The Government model properly field stripped.

MAGAZINE DISASSEMBLY

The magazine should be properly disassembled and cleaned. The follower is generally best left inside the magazine to avoid bending the lips. It is very important that the magazine spring be replaced in the proper direction, meaning the upward angle on the top of the spring should mate with the upward angle of the magazine follower. The spring should be inspected for shortness when compared to a new, full-powered spring (I recommend you replace the springs every three months in magazines left loaded). When replacing the base pad and retainer plate in the bottom of the magazine, inspect for cracks and make sure that the retainer plate securely locks the base pad onto the magazine.

OFFICERS MODEL DISASSEMBLY

Various models of 1911s require different disassembly procedures. For example, a Colt Officers model modified with a reinforced spring plug and one-piece guide rod assembly can be disassembled as follows.

Remove the magazine, empty and confirm the condition of the chamber, and lock the slide to the rear. The operator will find a hole in the forward portion of the guide rod in which he should insert a small crosspin, Allen wrench, or paper clip before gently allowing the slide to move forward until it stops. At this point, the slide stop tab will be nearly aligned with the half-moon disassembly notch on the slide and the slide stop can be completely removed. Now the entire barrel/bushing/slide and spring assemblies can be removed from the front of the frame. The guide rod/spring plug assembly can then be removed from the rear of the slide as a complete unit. The bushing can now be turned to expose its locking lug and be pulled out the front of the slide along with the barrel. No further disassembly is normally necessary for routine cleaning. Officers model operators with a reinforced spring plug/guide rod/barrel bushing system will want to have access to a crosspin capable of allowing easy disassembly.

COMPENSATED 1911 DISASSEMBLY

Remove the magazine, empty the chamber, and check and recheck the pistol to confirm that it is completely unloaded. If your pistol has a two-piece guide rod, loosen it approximately three turns. This is done by using an Allen wrench in the bottom hole in the front of the compensator. If your two-piece guide rod does not have an Allen socket, lock the slide open and find an approximately one-eighth of an inch hole in the guide rod just behind the compensator. Put a punch or similar device through the hole and loosen it by turning it counterclockwise. Turn the guide rod all the way out the front of the compensator with your fingers. Rods with Allen-style holes in the tip can be left intact and removed when you remove the slide from the front of the pistol, which will help you retain the spring while removing the slide. Rods with holes in them should be completely removed first, then remove the slide. Be sure to wrap your fingers around the bottom of the slide before removing it from the frame in order

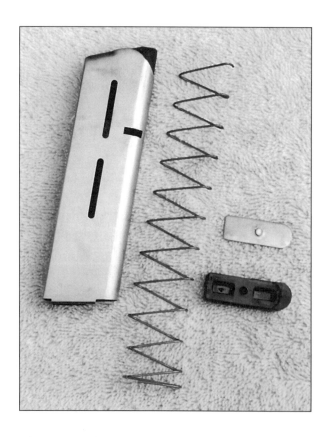

The magazine disassembled.

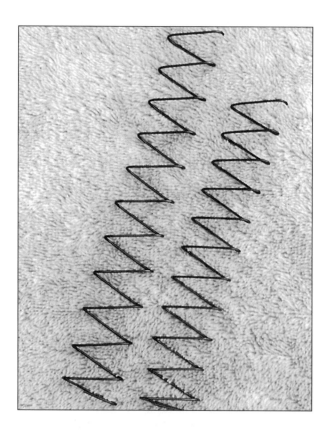

Long-term loaded magazines can result in spring set.

to retain the spring. Remove the slide from the frame by aligning the slide to a point where the slide stop can be pushed out of the small half-moon disassembly notch on the left side of the slide. Align the notch with the rear of the slide stop, then remove the slide stop by pushing with your finger on the slide stop crosspin protruding out the right side of the frame. Push it out while holding the notch in alignment with the rear of the slide stop. Holding this alignment is best accomplished by gripping the pistol in the strong hand with the web of the hand underneath the beavertail and four fingers over the top of the slide to hold it steady.

Remove the slide stop from the left side and let the slide go forward slowly, then push the slide forward and off of the frame. Wrap your fingers around the underside of the slide as it comes off of the frame to capture the recoil spring. Slowly release the recoil spring with one hand and maintain the release with the other hand. Once tension is released, remove it from the underside of the slide. If you remove the slide with the two-piece guide rod in place, hold your hand over the guide rod and spring. Keep the rod straight and unscrew the front piece of the rod with an Allen wrench, then remove the front half of the rod through the front of the compensator. The spring and the rear half of the rod will come out the rear underside of the slide. Set the spring and the rod aside. Hold the slide upside down in your weak hand and pivot the rear of the barrel upward (out of the locking lug recesses). Remove the barrel and compensator assembly by pulling it through the front of the slide after making sure the link is in its forward position. Cone barrels will pull out of the end of the slide at this point. Barrels with bushings need to be pulled forward approximately an inch so the bushing can be viewed. Push the spring plug deeper into the slide while turning the bushing with a plastic bushing wrench with the top half cut to fit over the barrel. Support the wrench arms with your fingers while turning until the bushing lug has been turned out of its slot. Remove the barrel through the front of the slide. If the bushing is tightly fitted, lightly tap it out with the barrel by gently pulling forward on the barrel comp assembly. (If done correctly, only light pressure is needed.) No further disassembly should be required to clean the pistol under normal conditions. Detailed cleaning by a pistolsmith should be done if the pistol has been seriously contaminated.

Removal of the firing pin, extractor, and related Series 80 parts should be left to the competent pistolsmith, because improper reassembly of these parts can lead to malfunctions and even the pistol firing when a cartridge is chambered. If the firing pin is improperly locked forward with the firing pin block, it can result in the firing pin protruding from the firing pin hole in the breech face. If the firing pin is not allowed to retract into its proper position inside the slide before a cartridge is chambered, the protruding firing pin may make contact with the primer and possibly discharge the cartridge.

THE MAINTENANCE HABIT

You should get into the habit of doing routine maintenance on your pistol and related equipment as you would any other piece of precision equipment. Clean your pistol at least every 400 rounds during practice fire, and always keep your pistol and equipment clean if you are planning on carrying it as a defensive sidearm.

Proper cleaning procedures and equipment are essential. Forget the salesman's hype about wonder equipment that never needs preventative maintenance. Maintain your gear. Use the correct size screwdrivers and proper bore brushes, bore cleaner, lubricant, and cleaning solution. Shooters who fire lead bullets will have additional concerns and must clean their leaded bores thoroughly. Failure to clean the leaded bore and chamber area can adversely affect the pistol's performance.

What To Use
Use only quality cleaning products. Shooter's Choice and Hoppe's are effective bore cleaners, and Break Free or FP-10 have long been known to be quality lubricants. Lead-free cloth is also a very useful

item when cleaning out stubborn leading problems in the bore. Outers Foul Out electronic bore cleaner also works well, although it is expensive. WD-40 is not recommended for cleaning or lubricating your pistol; it is unnecessary and has a good chance of later killing the primers in your cartridges.

Anyone who has shot an autopistol of any kind in an extended practice session, especially with lead bullets, knows how filthy the gun gets. You can spend hours cleaning a single pistol if you do it by hand with a rag and Q-tips or similar method. I have found that a more productive way is to use a quality aerosol cleaning solution, such as Gun Scrubber, which works well in the removal of powder residue and dirty lubricant. When applying aerosol solvent it is best to carefully avoid the pistol's wooden stocks or remove them altogether to prevent their being damaged. One should also avoid night sight inserts because a powerful solvent like Gun Scrubber will make any plastic or varnish coated materials tacky. In the case of clear night insert ampule covers, the solvent's action can give them a slightly milky appearance even after it has dried off, which reduces visibility through them. Even though some night insert companies advertise their night sights as being dunk-tank durable, the harshness of solvents can vary widely and occasionally produce adverse effects. Dunk tank cleaning of plastic parts or components with night inserts installed should be avoided. Solvents can also act upon any parts with Loc-Tite applied and reduce the product's ability to hold. This is especially true in the area of grip screw bushings on the 1911's frame. If a grip screw bushing is Loc-Tited instead of staked, it may come out of the frame when the grip screw is loosened to remove the pistol's stock. A bushing coming out with a screw can lead to damaged threads if proper procedure is not followed to replace the bushing. Although one can simply grip the bushing and back out the grip screw, this typically results in destruction of the bushing. A more effective and less destructive method is to thoroughly degrease the threads in the pistol's frame and bushing and put a small amount of red #271 Loc-Tite on the bushing threads only—avoiding the grip screw threads—and carefully turning the bushing back into the frame while taking care not to cross thread it. Once the Loc-Tite has cured between the frame and the grip screw bushing for 24 hours, one can normally back out the grip screw without dislodging the bushing. (Hex head grip screws are preferred because they are less susceptible to damage than slotted head grip screws when using an even slightly improperly fitted screwdriver.)

For the most part, a quality aerosol solvent will work very well in the overall initial cleaning of your autopistol. Followed up by compressed air and toothbrush action on heavily caked areas, another application of Gun Scrubber will make short work of most cleaning chores. The most caked-on areas, can easily be cleaned by using a bronze brush and a toothbrush dipped in bore cleaner. Gun Scrubber or a similar solvent can then be used again to clean up the bore cleaner and the crud that loosened up. (Be sure to use eye protection, gloves, and adequate ventilation when using any solvent, with or without compressed air.)

When cleaning the breech face area, one should be careful to thoroughly clean around the extractor hook with a gentle scrubbing motion, taking care not to bend the extractor and not to induce an unnecessary amount of solvent or lubricant into the firing pin hole. This material can drain back out of the firing pin hole and onto the primer of a chambered cartridge when the pistol is pointing downward in the holster. Thoroughly clean any lubricant or bore cleaner out of this area with the Gun Scrubber.

When cleaning the bore, make sure you clean it from the chamber end to the muzzle end with the proper sized brush. Push the brush all the way through the barrel and pull it all the way back out of the chamber to avoid damage to the rifling. Only quality bronze bristle brushes should be used; avoid stainless steel brushes because of potential damage to the bore. Be sure to thoroughly clean the chamber area; a dirty chamber can cause malfunctions, especially when lead bullets are used, which can leave lead residue in the front portion of the chamber.

Equipping yourself with the proper cleaning equipment to do a thorough job can normally be done quite inexpensively. A compact, portable, field cleaning kit makes a handy traveling companion.

For general home cleaning, the shooter should have a variety of toothbrushes, dental picks, bronze bore brushes, a bronze chamber brush, quality lubricant, a lead-free cloth or other lead cleaner, bore cleaner, bushing wrenches, clean soft rags, safety glasses, and a ventilated area.

Once the pistol is properly scrubbed and blown off with high-pressure Gun Scrubber and compressed air, the pistol will be bone dry and will need to be relubricated.

Important points for lubrication are the locking recesses inside the slide, outside of the barrel, slide rails, frame rails, disconnector (the small button that protrudes out of the frame behind the magazine well), barrel link, slide stop crosspin, guide rod, and barrel bushing. After these points have been lubricated, the slide should be cycled about a dozen times and the outside of the pistol thoroughly wiped off with a clean rag. The Gun Scrubber or other aerosol cleaning solution may leave what appears to be a water-stained appearance on the outside of the pistol, which will wipe away with an oily rag.

Break Free and FP-10 lubricants have a very wide ranging operating temperature, so they will work very well in most weather conditions. Running the pistol dry (without lubrication) is not recommended. If you are concerned about very dusty or very cold conditions, you should use at least a light dry lubrication. Dry lube doesn't offer the best lubrication and will probably be unnecessary unless the weather conditions are extreme. I have noted no sluggishness problems when using Break Free or FP-10 lubricants in conditions as cold as minus 70 degrees Fahrenheit (with wind chill) and minus 30 degrees air temp. If you are functional in the cold, it's probably not too cold for the pistol to function with proper lubrication. When the outside of the pistol is kept dry, the dust attraction problem is almost nonexistent. Routine maintenance and compressed air dusting of the pistol will keep dirt and lint out of the small, tight areas of the pistol.

Be sure to keep your ammunition clean, dry, and away from any lubricants or solvents; oils on your ammunition can result in misfires. Also, keep your chamber, bore, and breech face clean and dry to ensure that they don't allow oil to contaminate your ammunition.

This basic field stripping, cleaning, and lubrication program should be followed on a regular basis. Be sure to remove the magazine and empty the chamber, and double check it before field stripping. If you have any questions, consult your manual or pistolsmith.

Different pistols are fitted to different tolerances, have different options, and require different amounts of effort to disassemble. A pistol carried for self-defense should be capable of being disassembled under field conditions with few or no tools and perhaps a bit of improvisation. For example, in the case of the 1911 with its snug barrel bushing, you could use the plastic magazine base pad to gain the additional light force necessary to properly turn the bushing for disassembly. A knowledgeable shooter will not only be able to accomplish this under field conditions, but will be able to do so without marring the pistol's finish or losing the recoil spring plug. The operator should cup a finger over the spring plug (without covering the muzzle) while pointing the pistol into a plug containment area (not in the air) before turning the bushing to free the plug. (Under field conditions, holding the pistol close to soft ground with the muzzle downward will allow the plug to be located if it should happen to spring free.) A pistol without a guide rod can simply be unloaded, the slide slightly retracted, and the slide stop removed, thus allowing the slide assembly to be removed as a unit. The recoil spring and short guide can be removed from the rear underside of the slide. Then the barrel, plug, and barrel bushing can all be removed without dealing with any spring pressure.

Shooters who decide to carry a pistol that isn't easily field stripped may require a specialized tool or two to complete disassembly and should have these tools available at all times. In most cases this simply means carrying an item such as a bushing wrench head, a guide rod crosspin, or Allen wrench. These items are so small and handy that they can easily be carried in one's wallet.

Substantial force shouldn't be required to disassemble your 1911. Proper technique and experience should be all that is required.

General field stripping of the pistol is normally all the average shooter need do. Once field stripped, most of the internals can be blown clean. Unqualified persons should not go into the frame workings or

Series 80 slide workings because the parts can be mistakenly reassembled in a very unsafe manner and in some cases make the pistol nonfunctional. Pistols with deactivated safeties won't be worked on by reputable pistolsmiths unless the work involves correcting the problem. The Series 80 safety design is quite functional and provides a reliable failsafe. Do not deactivate the system.

A pistol that is carried for self-defense or as a duty weapon should have an in-depth cleaning by a competent pistolsmith any time it is seriously contaminated, such as being dropped in salt water or given a mud bath. This would be an opportunity to check for small part corrosion and to check out all of the relevant adjustments inside the pistol, such as extractor tension, trigger pull, sear engagement, and spring functions, and be given a full safety check.

Shock buff replacements vary from pistol to pistol and should be examined every time the pistol is disassembled. If the shock buff becomes cut, replace it. (An improperly maintained shock buff could be cut and separate inside the pistol and cause a malfunction.) I only recommend shock buffs for Government model or longer pistols, not in the Commander or Officers models, because the buff does slightly shorten the slide stroke. If your shock buff is cut, you don't have a suitable replacement, and immediate use is required, operate the pistol without the shock buff. A shock buff is designed to cushion the recoil impact the pistol generates when firing full-powered ammunition, but the pistol will still function reliably without the buff and without damaging the gun, unless extended firing of full-powered loads is done on a very regular basis.

To be thorough on your 1911 maintenance schedule, all other springs should be changed every 5,000 rounds by a competent pistolsmith, because some are internal frame springs. Your knowledgeable pistolsmith can supply you with the correct spring rates for the load you are shooting. If you are unsure of the spring rates, be sure to ask, because improper or poor quality springs can result in malfunctions.

If you are unsure of the field stripping procedure for your pistol, contact your pistolsmith for advice. Don't force anything together or apart; get the proper instruction before you start disassembly. If you have any problems in maintaining your pistol, contact your smith before you go too far and possibly damage something. A reputable smith will give all the assistance necessary for you to completely understand your pistol. A properly cared for and maintained auto digesting proper standard-pressure ammunition should last you a lifetime. Take care of your equipment and it will take care you.

Good shooting!

Appendix

ASSOCIATIONS, TRAINING SOURCES, AND PERIODICALS

ASSOCIATIONS

International Practical Shooting Confederation (IPSC)
Box 811
Sedro Wooley, WA 98284

Practical Shooting International (PSI)
Box 62
Emmetsberg, IA 50336

Outstanding American Handgunner Awards Foundation (OAHAF)
6410 Pomona Rd.
Boise, ID 83704

American Gunsmithing Association (AGA)
P.O. Box 540638
Merritt Island, FL 32952

1911 Society
301 Oak St.
Quincy, IL 62301

American Pistolsmiths Guild
1449 Bluecrest Ln.
San Antonio, TX 78232

DEFENSIVE TRAINING

D & L Sports (Dave Lauck)
P.O. Box 651
Gillette, WY 82717-0651

Mark Lonsdale
P.O. Box 491261
Los Angeles, CA 90049

Jeff Cooper
PO Box 401
Paulden, AZ 86334

Michael D. Janich (self-defense and weapons instructor)
c/o Paladin Press
P.O. Box 1307
Boulder, CO 80306

Erik Remmen (knife instructor)
NWS Group-9
P.O. Box 7172
Olympia, WA 98507

Thunder Ranch (Clint Smith)
HCRI Box 53
Mt. Home, TX 78058

Massad Ayoob
Box 122
Concord, NH 03302

Walt Rauch
P.O. Box 510
Lafayette Hill, PA 19444

PERIODICALS AND BOOKS

Paladin Press
P.O. Box 1307
Boulder, CO 80306

National Tactical Officers Association (NTOA)
P.O. Box 529
Doylestown, PA 18901

Harris Publications
1115 Broadway
New York, NY 10010

American Survival Guide
Y-Visionary L.P.
265 S. Anita Dr., Suite 120
Orange, CA 92868-3310

American Handgunner & *Guns*
591 Camino De La Reina, #200
San Diego, CA 92108

Precision Shooting/Tactical Shooter
222 McKee St.
Manchester, CT 06040

GLOSSARY

ACP: automatic Colt pistol

action: the mechanism used to load, unload, and fire the weapon

barrel: the cylindrical tube through which a bullet travels

base pad: an object usually made of leather, plastic, or rubber that is placed on the bottom of a magazine to ensure proper seating

battery: the condition of a firearm's action when it is in firing position

bore: the inside diameter of a barrel

bullet: a shaped piece of metal fitted in a cartridge and shot from a firearm

butt: the blunt, thick, handlelike part of the handgun grasped by the hand, consisting of the frame and stocks

cannelure: a groove on a bullet or case to prevent bullet pushback

cant: to hold a firearm at an angle

cartridge: a cylindrical metal case containing the primer, powder, and bullet for a firearm.

chamber: the part of a gun that holds the cartridge(s)

checkering: a uniform rough pattern embossed into steel or wood to provide a better grip

cock: to raise the hammer of a gun into firing position

concealment: that which allows one to hide but which is not bulletproof

cover (noun): that which provides concealment and is bulletproof

double-action (DA) semiautomatic: a pistol designed to be carried hammer down with a round in the chamber. The first shot is fired by trigger cocking the hammer; the remaining cartridges are fired single action.

ejection port: the opening on the slide where the spent casing is ejected

ejector: the device within the action that kicks an empty casing from the action

extractor: the device that removes an empty case from the chamber

firearm: a hand-held weapon which is discharged by igniting a powder charge

firing pin: a pin that strikes the cartridge primer in the chamber of a firearm

FMJ: full metal jacket

follower: the platform inside the magazine which guides the ammunition upward

fouling: the depositing of bullet jacket metal or lead in the bore of a weapon, which is detrimental to accuracy and functioning

fps: feet per second

galling: roughness on two pieces of metal caused by rubbing the metal surfaces together; common on some stainless steel autoloaders

GM: a Government model 1911

grip safety: a device designed to prevent the handgun from being fired unless the handgun is properly held by the operator

grip: the manner in which you place your hand on the gun to steady the weapon

hammer: the part of the action, driven by the mainspring, which when actuated by the trigger causes the firing pin to strike the primer, igniting the powder charge

hangfire: a delay between the striking of the primer and the igniting of the powder charge

holdover (or under): compensating for the bullet's trajectory when the target being shot is at a distance other than that for which the weapon is zeroed

hollow point: a type of expanding bullet

IPSC: International Practical Shooting Confederation

JFP: jacketed flat point

JHP: jacketed hollow point

kick: recoil

load: the exact specifications for a cartridge, such as weight and caliber size. To load a weapon is to place a cartridge in the chamber.

magazine: a device for semiautomatic pistols that holds additional cartridges ready for use

magazine well: the hole in the butt of a pistol which holds the magazine.

magnum: a cartridge design intended to develop a higher velocity than other cartridges of the same bore diameter

mainspring: the spring which drives the firing mechanism of a firearm

misfire: a condition in which a cartridge fails to fire after its primer has been struck

MSH: mainspring housing

muzzle blast (flash): the release of gas from the muzzle following the bullet's departure from the barrel. It produces noise and often light, which is called muzzle flash.

offhand: a standing position with no artificial support

OM: an Officers model 1911

piece: a slang expression for any firearm

pistol: a handgun. Commonly used to describe a semiautomatic handgun.

power: in handguns, the force expended by a cartridge when fired

primer: ignition cap on the rear end of a cartridge

pushback: the result of light case tension allowing the bullet to become more deeply seated in the case during the feed cycle

range: the distance a bullet will travel before losing its initial momentum. A place for shooting at targets; the distance to a target.

recoil spring: the spring(s) in a semiautomatic weapon that returns the action to battery after discharge

recoil: the backward motion of the weapon resulting from the firing of a round, also known as *kick*

revolver: a handgun with chambers in a rotating cylinder for holding several cartridges that may be fired in succession

RN: round-nose, as in a round-nose bullet

round: a complete cartridge

round-nose: a bullet with a rounded frontal portion

sear: the part that holds the hammer in the cocked position

semiwadcutter: a long, blunt-nose bullet with a full-diameter shoulder that is designed to feed reliably and cut a clean hole in the target (SWC)

shock: the transfer of a bullet's kinetic energy to the mass of a target

sidearm: a pistol or revolver carried at the side or on a belt

sight radius: the distance between the front and rear sights

sight: any of several devices used to align the eye as nearly as possible with the trajectory of a firearm's bullet

sighting in: firing a weapon to determine a bullet's point-of-impact at a specified range in relation to sight hold; adjusting sights to intersect bullet impact and sight hold at a specific range

single-action (SA) automatic: a pistol designed to be carried with the hammer fully cocked, the safety in the on position, and a round in the chamber; each round must be fired with a pull of the trigger after the round has been chambered and the hammer manually cocked

single-action revolver: a revolver designed to fire only by manually thumb cocking the hammer, which rotates the cylinder for each shot

slide: the portion of a semiautomatic pistol that moves to chamber, fire, and eject a cartridge

small arms: firearms intended to be carried and operated by one person

stock: the wood or plastic portion of a firearm intended to be held by the hands to support the weapon

strong hand: the master hand used for firing the weapon

SWC: semiwadcutter

target: what you wish the bullet to strike

thumb safety (safety latch): a device which, when set, mechanically prevents the firing of a gun

trajectory: the flight path of a bullet

trigger: the finger piece of a handgun which, when pulled, releases the hammer

trigger guard: a usually curved piece of metal attached to a gun's frame which surrounds the trigger

wadcutter: a type of bullet commonly referred to in an abbreviated form as WC. It has a cylindrical shape with flat ends and is mainly used for match shooting with light powder charges.

weak hand: the hand used to support the master hand

zero: in shooting, the sight setting at which point-of-impact and point-of-aim coincide at a given range

ABOUT THE AUTHOR

Dave Lauck is a veteran front line police officer with extensive experience in practical firearms, firearm instruction, gunsmithing, SWAT, police countersniper training, special investigations, and patrolling. A certified armorer, he was unanimously selected to be the 1996 recipient of the Excellence in Craft Award presented by the American Gunsmithing Association. Lauck has been recognized as one of America's top five pistolsmiths and has been inducted into Club 100 and the American Pistolsmiths Guild, which represents America's top gunsmiths. He has crafted eight consecutive world championship presentation pistols that have been presented at various shooting events. His customized 1911 crafted for Jeff Cooper is in the Buffalo Bill Museum as a representative piece of firearms history. He is a founding life member of the 1911 Society, a life member of the NRA, and a member of the American Gunsmithing Association, American Pistolsmiths Guild, Police Marksmans Association, Outstanding American Handgunner Awards Foundation, and American Sniper Association. Lauck is also a staff writer for *Tactical Shooter* and *American Gunsmith*.

Lauck is a NRA-certified handgun, shotgun, and long-range rifle instructor and POST-certified practitioner/lecturer in SWAT and countersniper tactics. He holds expert firearms ratings and has received numerous awards in competitive practical shooting, including team captain at the 1991 World Championship Tactical Match, first place in the 1990 World Champion Tactical Rifle Event, top 10 percent finisher overall in the Three Gun World Championship in 1990, first place in the 600-meter NRA Long Range Rifle Instructor Shoot Off in 1988, first place SAA Countersniper Shoot Off in 1987, SDHD Two Gun Combat Match Police champion in 1986, Northwest Regional Champion in 1985, and Wyoming Tactical Division winner in 1995. In 1996 and 1997 he was awarded outstanding shooter awards.

He is the founder of D & L Sports Custom Firearms, Inc., and Small Arms Training Academy (SATA) in Gillette, Wyoming. He teaches his performance-proven shooting principles to law enforcement and military personnel, as well as qualified civilians. D & L Sports S.A.T.A. hosts the annual tactical marksman's match to provide a proving ground for the best in tactical weapons and techniques. For more information contact:

D & L Sports
Custom Firearms and Small Arms Training Academy
P.O. Box 651
Gillette, Wyoming 82717-0651
Phone: (307) 686-4008 Fax: (307) 686-5093